EVERYTHING YOU NEED TO KNOW ABOUT
AMERICAN HISTORY
HOMEWORK

Anne Zeman and Kate Kelly

An Irving Place Press Book

**SCHOLASTIC
REFERENCE**

New York   Toronto   London   Auckland   Sydney

Cover design, Charles Kreloff; Cover illustration, James Steinberg
Interior design, Bennett Gewirtz, Gewirtz Graphics, Inc.; Interior illustration, Moffit Cecil

For their assistance in the preparation of maps, charts, and graphics, grateful acknowledgment to
Thomas Simpfendoerfer, Cathy Bontempo, Karin Martin, and Carla Alpert.
For their assistance in the preparation of this manuscript, grateful acknowledgment to Betty
Holmes, Director of UFT's Dial-A-Teacher; Vincent Ridge; and Carmen Edgerly. Dial-A-Teacher is
a collaborative program of the United Federation of Teachers and the New York City Board of
Education.

Grateful acknowledgment is made to:
  FPG International, for permission to reprint photographs on pages 30, 58, 80, and 81.
  The Library of Congress, for permission to reprint photographs on pages 32, 33, 36, 45, 47, 48, 55,
    59, 62-63, 65, 70, 71, 75, 76-77, 87, 92, 93, 94, 96, 97, 101, 102, and 103.
  The Scholastic Picture Research Department for permission to reprint photographs on pages 55,
    69, 78, 95, 99, 100, 103 (photograph, Hideki Tojo), and 104.
  The National Portrait Gallery, Smithsonian Institution, for the photograph of Frederick Douglass
    on page 55.
  The National Park Service for the photograph on page 78.

Illustrations copyright (c) 1994, 1993 by Scholastic Inc.

Library of Congress Cataloging-in-Publication Data

Zeman, Anne, 1951-
    Everything you need to know about American history homework / Anne
        Zeman and Kate Kelly.
        p.   cm. — (Scholastic homework reference series)
    Includes index.
    ISBN 0-590-49363-9
    1. United States—History—Miscellanea—Juvenile literature.
    2. Homework—Juvenile literature. [1. United States—History.
    2. Homework.] I. Kelly, Kate. II. Title. III. Series.
    E178.3.Z45   1994
    973—dc20   93-46359
                                                                     CIP
                                                                     AC

12 11   9/9

CONTENTS

INTRODUCTION

It's homework time—but you have questions. Just how did your teacher ask you to do the assignment? You need help, but your parents are busy, and you can't reach your classmate on the phone. Where can you go for help?

What Questions Does This Book Answer?

In *Everything You Need to Know About American History Homework*, you will find a wealth of information, including the answers to ten of the most commonly asked American history homework questions.*

1. What was Columbus looking for on his trip in 1492? What Columbus sought and what he found are described on page 6.

2. What is Latin America and why is it called that? Why are some North Americans called Anglos? The origins of these New World names are found on page 9.

3. What were the Articles of Confederation, and why did they fail? To learn about the early U.S. government — and the Articles of Confederation — see pages 28-29.

4. What is Manifest Destiny? Manifest Destiny and the important U.S. policy statement it inspired are described on page 48.

5. What were the causes and results of the Civil War? Many of the complex causes and results of the Civil War are listed in easy-to-use charts and a chronology on pages 60-64.

6. What caused the growth of labor unions? The rise of labor and labor unions are the topic of pages 75-76.

7. What were the causes and results of the Spanish-American War? The Spanish-American War is discussed on pages 80-81.

8. How did the United States get involved in World Wars I and II? U.S. involvement in both wars is described in detail — complete with chronology sections — on pages 84-90 and 98-107.

9. What caused the Great Depression, and how did it end? The Great Depression is the topic of pages 95-97.

10. What was the Cold War? The Cold War is explained on page 109.

* According to Dial-A-Teacher

What Is the Scholastic Homework Reference Series?

The Scholastic Homework Reference Series is a set of unique reference resources written especially to answer the homework questions of fourth, fifth, and sixth graders. The series provides ready information to answer commonly asked homework questions in a variety of subjects. Here you'll find facts, charts, definitions, and explanations, complete with examples and illustrations that will supplement schoolwork colorfully, clearly—and comprehensively.

A Note to Parents

The information for the Scholastic Homework Reference Series was gathered from current textbooks, national curricula, and the invaluable assistance of the UFT Dial-A-Teacher staff. Dial-A-Teacher, a collaborative program of the United Federation of Teachers and the New York City Board of Education, is a telephone service available to elementary school students in New York City. Telephone lines are open during the school term from 4:00 to 7:00 p.m., Monday to Thursday, by dialing 212-777-3380. Because of Dial-A-Teacher's success in New York City, similar organizations have been established in other communities across the country. Check to see if there's a telephone homework service in your area.

It's important to support your children's efforts to do homework. Welcome their questions and see that they are equipped with a well-lighted desk or table, pencils, paper, and any other books or equipment—such as rulers, calculators, reference or text books, and so on—that they may need. You might also set aside a special time each day for doing homework, a time when you're available to answer questions that may arise. But don't do your children's homework for them. Remember, homework should create a bond between school and home. It is meant to enhance on a daily basis the lessons taught at school, and to promote good work and study habits. Although it is gratifying to have your children present flawless homework papers, the flawlessness should be a result of your children's explorations and efforts—not your own.

The Scholastic Homework Reference Series is designed to help your children complete their homework on their own to the best of their abilities. If they're stuck, you can use these books with them to find answers to troubling homework problems. And, remember, when the work is done—praise your children for a job well done.

U.S. States and Capitals

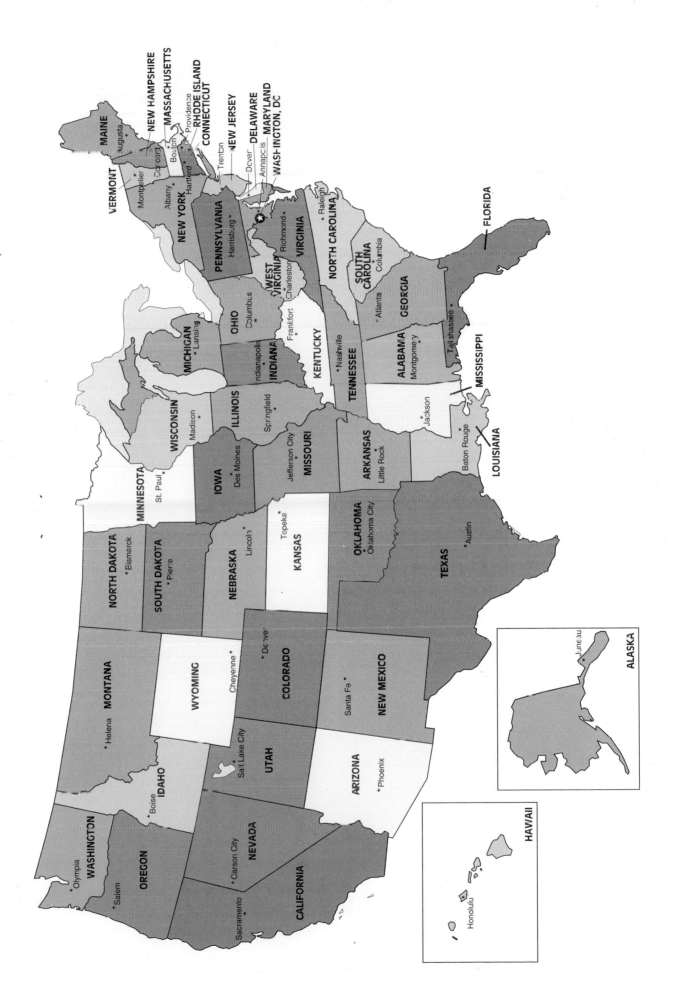

MAINE
*Augusta

NEW HAMPSHIRE
Concord

MASSACHUSETTS
Boston *

VERMONT
Montpelier *

RHODE ISLAND
Providence

CONNECTICUT
Hartford *

NEW YORK
Albany *

NEW JERSEY
Trenton

DELAWARE
Dover

MARYLAND
Annapolis *

WASHINGTON, DC

PENNSYLVANIA
Harrisburg *

NORTH CAROLINA
Raleigh *

VIRGINIA
Richmond *

WEST VIRGINIA
Charleston *

OHIO
Columbus *

SOUTH CAROLINA
Columbia

FLORIDA

GEORGIA
Atlanta *

MICHIGAN
Lansing *

KENTUCKY
Frankfort *

TENNESSEE
Nashville *

ALABAMA
Montgomery *

Tallahassee *

INDIANA
Indianapolis *

MISSISSIPPI

ILLINOIS
Springfield *

WISCONSIN
Madison *

MISSOURI
Jefferson City *

ARKANSAS
Little Rock *

Jackson *

LOUISIANA
Baton Rouge *

MINNESOTA
St. Paul *

IOWA
Des Moines *

NORTH DAKOTA
Bismarck *

SOUTH DAKOTA
Pierre *

NEBRASKA
Lincoln *

KANSAS
Topeka *

OKLAHOMA
Oklahoma City *

TEXAS
Austin *

MONTANA
Helena *

WYOMING
Cheyenne *

COLORADO
Denver *

NEW MEXICO
Santa Fe *

IDAHO
Boise *

UTAH
Salt Lake City *

ARIZONA
Phoenix *

WASHINGTON
Olympia *

OREGON
Salem *

NEVADA
Carson City *

CALIFORNIA
Sacramento *

ALASKA
Juneau *

HAWAII
Honolulu

NORTH AMERICA BEFORE 1775

1 The First Americans

Over the Land Bridge

The first people to live in North America came from Asia. They arrived 10,000 to 30,000 years ago. At that time, Asia and North America were connected by a bridge of land. The first people who crossed this land bridge were probably hunting for bison and woolly mammoths. They followed herds into what is now Northern Canada. Eventually people spread throughout North, Central, and South America. Today, these people are called *Native Americans* or *American Indians*.

SIBERIA

ALASKA

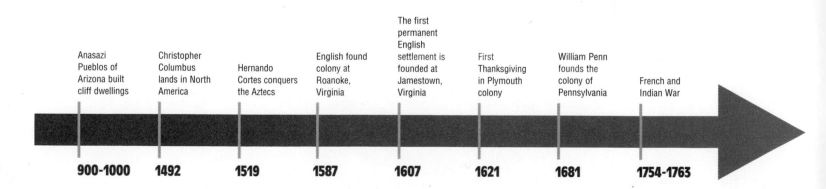

Anasazi Pueblos of Arizona built cliff dwellings	Christopher Columbus lands in North America	Hernando Cortes conquers the Aztecs	English found colony at Roanoke, Virginia	The first permanent English settlement is founded at Jamestown, Virginia	First Thanksgiving in Plymouth colony	William Penn founds the colony of Pennsylvania	French and Indian War
900-1000	1492	1519	1587	1607	1621	1681	1754-1763

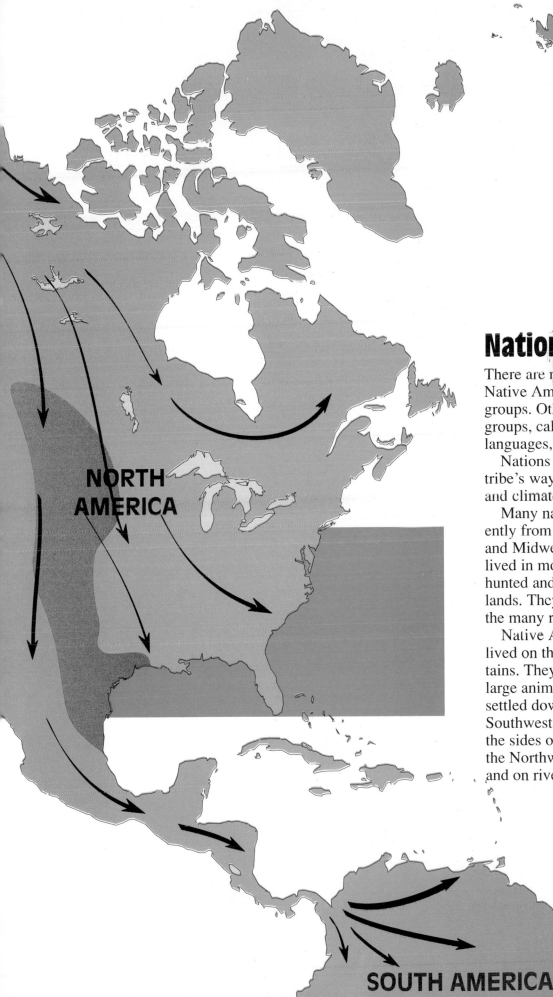

NORTH AMERICA

SOUTH AMERICA

Nations and Tribes

There are many different groups of Native Americans. Some live in small groups. Others are city dwellers. Large groups, called *nations*, have their own languages, customs, and religions.

Nations are divided into *tribes*. Each tribe's way of life is shaped by the land and climate in which it lives.

Many nations today live quite differently from their ancestors. In the East and Midwest, Native Americans once lived in mountains and forests. They hunted and gathered food in the woodlands. They also fished in the ocean and the many rivers and farmed the land.

Native Americans in the West once lived on the prairies and in the mountains. They were hunters who followed large animals, mainly buffalo. Some settled down and began to farm. In the Southwest, some even dug cities into the sides of cliffs. Native Americans in the Northwest used to live in the forests and on rivers and lakes.

Some Native American Tribes and Where They Lived, Around 1650

Native Americans of the North and Northeast

Abenaki	Illinois	Montauk	Pequot
Algonquin	Iroquois	Narraganset	Potawatomi
Conestoga	Kickapoo	Ojibway	Sauk
Delaware	Menominee	Oneida	Seneca
Erie	Miami	Ottawa	Susquehanna
Fox	Mohawk	Pawtuxet	Wampanoag
Huron	Mohican	Pennacook	Winnebago

Native Americans of the Southeast

Apalachee	Cherokee	Natchez	Timucoa
Attacapa	Chickasaw	Powhatan	Tuscarora
Biloxi	Choctaw	Quapaw	Tutelo
Calusa	Creek	Saponi	
Catawba	Croatan	Shawnee	

Native Americans of the Plains

Arapaho	Comanche	Nez Perce	Sioux (Dakota)
Arikara	Cree	Omaha	Ute
Brea	Crow	Osage	Wichita
Blackfoot	Iowa	Oto	Caddo Mandan
Pawnee	Cheyenne	Missouri	Shoshone

Native Americans of the Southwest

Apache	Mohave	Pomo	Walapai
Cochimi	Navaho	Pueblo	Yuma
Hopi	Paiute	Serrano	Zuni
Lagunero	Papago	Taos	

Native Americans of the Northwest

Bannock	Haida*	Paloos	Tsimshian*
Chinook	Makah	Tenino	Yakima
Duwamish	Nisqualli	Tillamook	Yuki
Flathead	Nootka	Tlingit*	

* These tribes lived in the area that is now Alaska.

MAKAH
DUWAMISH
NOOTKA
NISQUALLI
TILLAMOOK
YAKIMA
PALOOS
FLATHEAD
CHINOOK
TENINO
NEZ PERCE
Snake River
BANNOCK
SHASTA
NORTHERN PAIUTE
SHOSHONE
YUKI
GREAT SALT LAKE
POMO
UTE
PAIUTE
River
Colorado
HOPI
WALAPAI
NAVAHO
TAOS
SERRANO
MOHAVE
ZUNI
YUMA

Pacific Ocean

COCHIMI
PAPAGO

Lake
Winnipeg

BLACKFOOT

OJIBWAY

HURON

CREE

Lake
Superior

ABENAKI

OTTAWA

MENOMINEE

Lake
Huron

HURON

MOHAWK

PENNACOOK

CROW

MANDAN

OJIBWAY

SAUK

ONEIDA

MOHICAN

WAMPANOAG

SIOUX

SIOUX

FOX

L. Ontario

SUSQUEHANNA

PAWTUXET

WINNEBAGO

Lake
Michigan

ALGONQUIN

SENECA

NARRAGANSET

KICKAPOO

POTAWATOMI

IROQUOIS

PEQUOT

ARIKARA

Missouri River

IOWA

L. Erie

MONTAUK

ARAPAHO

BREA
PAWNEE

OMAHA

ERIE

CONESTOGA

DELAWARE

OTO

ILLINOIS

CHEYENNE

MISSOURI

MIAMI

River

Ohio

CROATAN

WICHITA

TUTELO

POWHATAN

Arkansas

OSAGE

SHAWNEE

SAPONI

PAWNEE

TUSCARORA

PUEBLO

River

QUAPAW

CHICKASAW

CHEROKEE

CATAWBA

Mississippi River

APACHE

COMANCHE

Red

CADDO

Atlantic Ocean

River

CHOCTAW

CREEK

Rio

NATCHEZ

ATTACAPA

BILOXI

APALACHEE

TIMUCOA

Grande

GUNERO

CALUSA

AZTEC

Gulf of Mexico

St. Lawrence River

St

5

2 European Explorers Find a New World

In 1492, Native American life began to change dramatically. **Christopher Columbus**, an Italian who was captain of three Spanish ships, "discovered" what Europeans called a *New World*. He thought he had reached the Spice Islands near India. He called the people he met "Indians." Soon after, other European nations sent explorers to the Americas.

FIVE REASONS FOR EUROPEAN EXPLORATION

1. **To find a new passage to the Far East for trade**
2. **To find gold, silver, precious gems, and other valuables**
3. **To claim new lands for their countries**
4. **To convert people to Christianity**
5. **For adventure**

At first, Native Americans welcomed the Europeans. They introduced the Europeans to tomatoes, corn, potatoes, and tobacco. Europeans introduced Native Americans to guns, sugarcane, and horses. They also brought diseases new to the Americas—the common cold, measles, and smallpox, to name a few—which killed many Native Americans.

When Europeans began to explore and later settle in North America, they used guns to take whatever they wanted. They thought they had the right to do this. When they built villages and cities, they often cleared forests. These forests were the homes of many of the wild animals the Native Americans hunted.

Some groups, like the Cherokee, took on European ways, but the settlers wanted their land anyway. Most tribes that survived were forced to move west. Today, most of the remaining American Indians live there. Some have sued the government to repay them for the land that was taken from them or granted to them by treaties that were broken.

Christopher Columbus sailed over the course of several weeks, finally to land in the New World. Columbus's expedition sailed on three ships, the *Nina, Pinta,* and *Santa Maria.* These ships had hulls and masts of wood with cloth sails. By today's standards, the *Nina, Pinta,* and *Santa Maria* were very small and very slow.

Exploration Routes

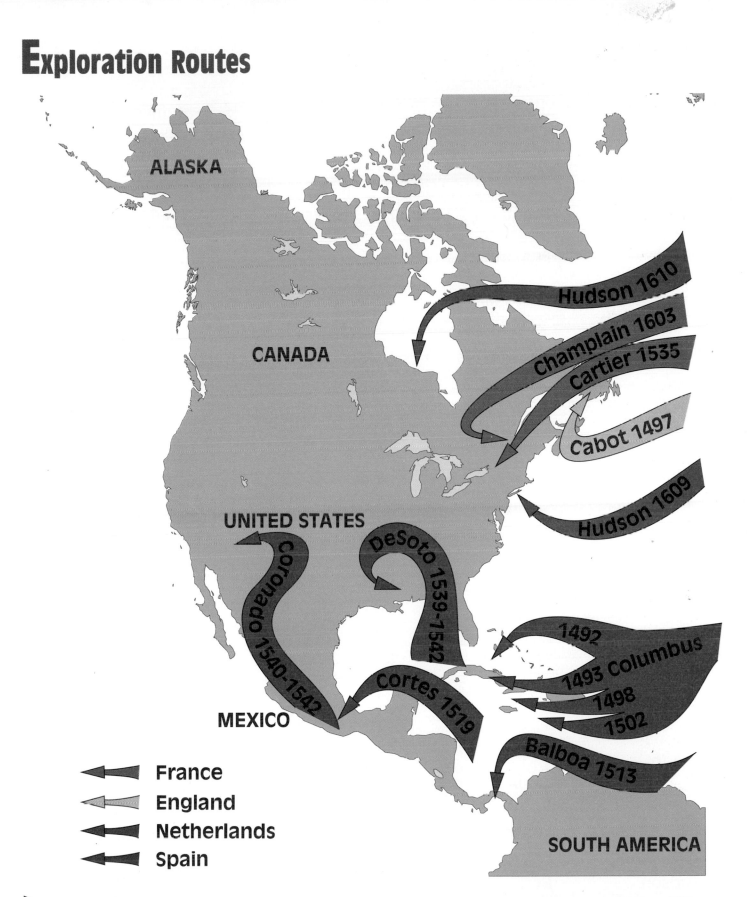

ALASKA

CANADA

UNITED STATES

MEXICO

SOUTH AMERICA

Hudson 1610

Champlain 1603

Cartier 1535

Cabot 1497

Hudson 1609

Coronado 1540-1542

DeSoto 1539-1542

Cortes 1519

Balboa 1513

1492

1493 Columbus

1498

1502

France

England

Netherlands

Spain

Amerigo Vespucci *was a merchant in Italy who sold supplies to Christopher Columbus and made maps of the voyages of Columbus and other explorers. Between 1499 and 1502, he explored the Amazon River and the coast of South America. Unlike Columbus, Amerigo Vespucci realized that America was a separate continent and not a part of Asia. America was named for him in 1507 by a German mapmaker.*

Early European Explorers (in chronological order)

EXPLORERS	COUNTRY REPRESENTED	YEAR OF EXPLORATION	JOURNEY
Leif Ericson	Vikings (Norway)	about 1000	Newfoundland
Bartolomeu Dias	Portugal	1487-1488	First European to round Cape of Good Hope at the southern tip of Africa
Christopher Columbus	Spain	1492	San Salvador and West Indies
John Cabot	England	1497	Greenland, Labrador, Newfoundland
Vasco da Gama	Portugal	1497-1498	First to reach India from Europe by sea
Amerigo Vespucci	Spain	1497-1502	South America and West Indies
Pedro Cabral	Portugal	1500	Sailed around Africa to India; Brazil
Vasco de Balboa	Spain	1513	Pacific Ocean
Ferdinand Magellan	Spain	1509-1522	First to sail around the globe
Juan Ponce de Leon	Spain	1513	Florida
Hernando Cortes	Spain	1519-1521	Aztec kingdom of Mexico
Giovanni da Verrazano	France	1524	Eastern coast of North America
Panfilo de Narvaez	Spain	1528	Florida and Mexico
Francisco Pizarro	Spain	1531	Inca empire of Peru
Jacques Cartier	France	1535	St. Lawrence River
Esteban and Father Marcos	Spain	1539	Canada and Quebec; Zuni pueblos of New Mexico
Hernando DeSoto	Spain	1539-1542	Mississippi River, American Southeast
Francisco de Coronado	Spain	1540-1542	American Southwest
Juan Rodriguez Cabrillo	Spain	1542	California
Sir Francis Drake	England	1577-1580	Around the world
Samuel de Champlain	France	1603-1609	The Great Lakes and Quebec
Henry Hudson	Netherlands	1609	Hudson River and Hudson Bay

3 Colonization of the Americas

Spain, France, and Britain sent explorers to the Americas. Later, they claimed huge territories and built colonies. (A *colony* is a settlement in a new land, often far away from the home country. *Colonists* are people who leave their country to settle in a colony.)

French explorers claimed the land from Canada through the Great Lakes, and down the Mississippi River to the Gulf of Mexico. They called this territory *New France*. By 1750, 70,000 to 75,000 French fur traders and missionaries lived in New France. They set up a few forts and moved from place to place. Native Americans taught them how to fish and trap animals. The missionaries wanted to win over the Native Americans to Christianity.

Spain claimed most of what is today Texas, New Mexico, Arizona, and California, as well as Mexico, where it conquered the Aztec Empire. Spain also established colonies in Central and South America.

Britain had colonies in the Caribbean and the thirteen colonies along the Atlantic coast of North America.

▶ *Spain established a fort at St. Augustine, Florida, in 1565. The city of St. Augustine is the oldest continuous settlement in North America.*

▶ *Today, Mexico, Central, and South America are often called* Latin America *because most of the region's people speak Spanish or Portuguese—two languages that grew out of Latin. English-speaking North Americans are sometimes called* Anglos, *from the Spanish word for English.*

The Thirteen British Colonies

New England

New Hampshire

Massachusetts

New York

Rhode Island

Connecticut

New Jersey

Middle Colonies

Pennsylvania

Delaware

Maryland

Southern Colonies

Virginia

North Carolina

South Carolina

Georgia

9

Early British Colonies

The Lost Colony of Roanoke

In the 1580s, *Elizabeth I* was queen of England. *Sir Walter Raleigh* tried to convince her to start some colonies in North America. Elizabeth was not eager, but she gave Raleigh some money and a *charter* (a piece of paper saying he had royal permission to build a colony). With some other people, he started a colony on an island near the Outer Banks of present-day North Carolina. They named the large area *Virginia* in honor of Elizabeth, who never married and was called the Virgin Queen. The island was named *Roanoke*.

Two groups tried to form a colony there before a third group was successful in 1587. A child was born that year named *Virginia Dare*. She was the first child of English parents born in the New World.

Virginia's grandfather, Governor *John White*, went back to England for more supplies. When he returned in 1591, all that was left of the settlement was a post on which the name *Croatan* was printed. White thought the settlers might have gone to live with the Croatan Indians, but the weather was too bad to find out. Croatan legend says the settlers became a part of their tribe. The English have always referred to them as the *Lost Colony*.

Jamestown, the Permanent English Settlement

In 1606, the British king, *James I*, gave to a group of businessmen a charter called the Virginia Company of London. They were supposed to establish a colony in Virginia and look for gold. The 120 people who arrived on May 14, 1607, founded the first successful English settlement in the Americas.

They settled near a river, which they named the James River for their king. Most of the settlers believed they could quickly find gold and return to England. But no gold was to be found. By December, more than half of the settlers had died from disease, starvation, or Native American attacks.

One of the remaining settlers, *John Smith*, took charge. He began trading with *Powhatan*, chief of the Powhatan tribe, for corn and beans for the starving settlers. Smith would not trade guns, so the Powhatans decided to kill him. Legend says that *Pocahontas*, Powhatan's daughter, convinced him to spare Smith's life.

The London Company continued to send supplies and more people to Virginia. *John Rolfe* arrived and began to grow tobacco in 1612. This was the first crop that could be sold in Europe. Tobacco, not gold, became the treasure of the Jamestown colony. In 1614, Rolfe married Pocahontas, assuring peace with the Powhatans. He took her to England, where she met the king and queen. She died there of smallpox, a disease for which she had no immunity.

Peace ended in 1622. The settlers wanted more land. They killed a Powhatan war chief. The Powhatans fought back, killing almost one-quarter of the settlers. The London Company went bankrupt, and Jamestown became a royal colony until it burned in 1698.

Life in the British Colonies

Settlers in the colonies had to support themselves on the land and in the climate where they settled. For example, many New England colonists made a living from fishing and shipbuilding. Others had small farms and shops. In the Middle colonies, where the soil and climate were better, farming was the main way of life. The climate was even better for farming in the Southern colonies, where crops grew almost all year.

New England

Most people in *New England* lived in towns or on small farms. New Englanders traded fish, lumber, and furs with other towns along the Atlantic coast. The Massachusetts towns of Salem and Boston were the main seaports for trade.

Middle Colonies

Many families in the *Middle colonies* lived on farms. Their chief crops were wheat, rye, oats, and barley, from which they made flour and bread. The Middle colonies were also a center of manufacturing. Here glass, leather goods and shoes, and barrels and containers were made. The Middle colonies also became known for their ironworks, including the manufacture of guns, axes, and tools. New York, New York, and Philadelphia, Pennsylvania, were their main ports.

Southern Colonies

In the *Southern colonies*, almost everyone made a living by farming. The chief crops were tobacco, rice, and indigo (a plant used to make dye). Most of the colonists had small farms and lived simply. Wealthy colonists owned huge plantations and slaves who did most of the work. Charleston, South Carolina, and Savannah, Georgia, were southern ports where cotton and slaves were traded.

Colonial Religion

The earliest English settlers in Virginia were members of the official Church of England, called *Anglicans*. Later, to Massachusetts, came *Puritans*, Protestants who wanted to reform or "purify" the Church of England. Pilgrims, Congregationalists, and Baptists all grew out of the Puritan movement. (Protestants are Christians who left the Roman Catholic Church in the 1500s.)

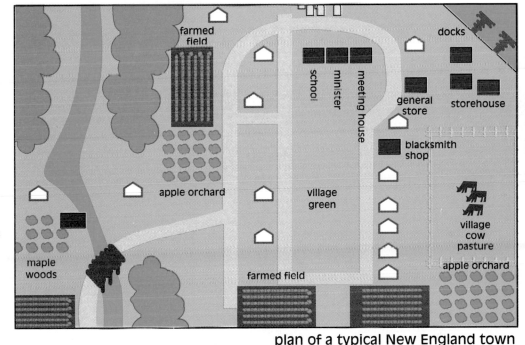

plan of a typical New England town

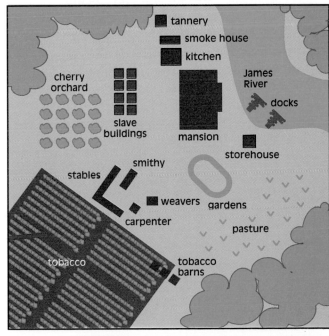

plan of a typical Southern plantation

Early African Americans

The first Africans were brought to America in 1619. A Dutch ship captain sold them to settlers in Jamestown. As the slave trade grew, the majority of slaves were brought to work on Southern *plantations*.

Almost every European country and African empire made huge profits from the slave trade. People were kidnapped, usually in West Africa, brought to the Americas, and separated from their families and friends. About 350,000 slaves were brought to America during the 1700s. By 1800, the African American population was more than one million, of which 893,000 were enslaved. There were three million slaves by 1850. Marriage was not legal among slaves. Any children born to them were considered the master's property.

Not all African Americans were slaves, however. Early on, "free blacks" established homes in North America, but they were not allowed to serve in the army nor, later, to vote. Free blacks often were unwelcome — even in church — so they later formed their own churches, schools, neighborhoods, and cultural organizations.

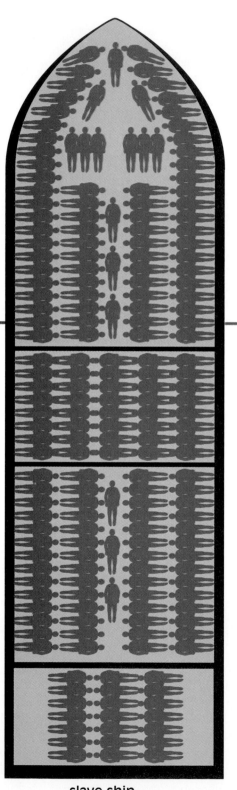

Africans were brought to the Americas on board crowded slave ships. Many died on these ships and others became too ill to be sold at auction upon their arrival in the New World.

slave ship

Some New World Personalities

Governor **William Bradford** was the second governor of the Plymouth Colony in Massachusetts. In 1621, he called for a Thanksgiving, in which Pilgrims celebrated the fall harvest with ninety Wampanoag warriors.

Anne Hutchinson, a Puritan who originally settled in Massachusetts, was ordered to leave the Massachusetts Bay Colony when she spoke out against church ministers. She moved to Rhode Island, founded by Roger Williams who was himself a Puritan dissenter. In Rhode Island, she was free to teach religion in public.

Montezuma

Queen Isabella of Spain provided **Christopher Columbus** with ships to make his journey of exploration. She hoped that Columbus's discoveries would bring Spain new trade and riches, most of which she expected to keep.

In 1739, sixteen-year-old **Eliza Lucas** was left in charge of her father's three plantations in South Carolina. She developed a new crop, **indigo**, which produced a blue dye used on cloth.

Montezuma was the last leader of the **Aztec Empire**, in present-day Mexico. He took power in 1502. In 1519, he welcomed the Spanish explorer **Hernando Cortés** to the Aztec city of Tenochtitlán. Cortes took Montezuma prisoner and, in two years, destroyed the Aztec Empire.

Popé was a Pueblo medicine man in the Southwest. In 1680, he led a successful revolt against the Spanish. He became a leader of the Pueblo tribe.

Squanto was a member of the Pawtuxet tribe, who taught the Pilgrims at the Plymouth colony in Massachusetts how to grow corn, hunt, and fish. Without his help, many Pilgrims would have died.

4 Beginnings of Democracy in the British Colonies

The London Company

In 1619, the London Company gave Virginia colonists a voice in their own government. The Company provided for a legislature of colonists to pass laws. This became the first representative government in North America. Called the **House of Burgesses** (in England, a burgess is the representative of a local government, or borough), it was patterned after British local governments.

The Mayflower Compact

In 1620, a group of people called Pilgrims wanted to separate from the Church of England. They and some other passengers set sail from Plymouth, England, on the **Mayflower**, headed toward Virginia, but the ship was blown off course and landed in Cape Cod Bay at a place the Pilgrims named for their home port, Plymouth. Before they landed, the Pilgrims signed the **Mayflower Compact**, an agreement that provided for a government and set of laws for the new Pilgrim colonists.

Town Meetings

In New England — Connecticut, Rhode Island, New Hampshire, and Massachusetts (which included Maine) — many community affairs were governed by town meetings held once or twice a year in which all eligible voters had a voice. Only white males who were members of the Congregational Church could vote, except in Rhode Island, where membership in the Congregational Church was not required. Town meetings were direct democracies because people spoke for themselves directly. However, they did elect officers to run the town between meetings. Town meetings are still held in some New England communities.

Pilgrim life was full of hardships. Rocky earth had to be cleared for farming, and cold winters often meant a scarcity of food. Laws and punishments for lawbreakers were sternly enforced, often using devices — such as the pillory — that had been used in England.

Founding of the Thirteen British Colonies

COLONY	YEAR FOUNDED	FOUNDED BY	CHIEF CROPS OR TRADE
NEW ENGLAND COLONIES			
Massachusetts			
Plymouth	1620	Pilgrims led by William Bradford	Fish, lumber, shipbuilding
Massachusetts Bay	1630	Puritans led by John Winthrop	Fish, lumber, shipbuilding
Rhode Island			
Providence	1636	Roger Williams, who left Massachusetts for religious reasons	Fish, lumber
Connecticut			
Hartford	1636	Thomas Hooker, who led a group from Massachusetts who wanted less government	Fish, lumber, shipbuilding
New Hampshire			
Rye	1623	Colonists who left Massachusetts for religious and political reasons	Fish, molasses
MIDDLE COLONIES			
New York			
New Amsterdam	1626	Dutch; English in 1664	Shipbuilding and trade
New Jersey			
	1664	Dutch and Swedish; Lord John Berkeley and Sir George Carteret were given the land in 1664 by the English Duke of York	Wheat, rye, oats
Pennsylvania			
Philadelphia	1681	William Penn as a safe place for Quakers	Shipbuilding and trade
Delaware	1682	William Penn	Tobacco
SOUTHERN COLONIES			
Virginia			
Jamestown (Chesapeake)	1607	Settlers led by John Smith from Virginia Company of London	Tobacco
Maryland			
Baltimore	1634	Lord Baltimore as a safe place for Catholics	Tobacco
North Carolina			
Albemarle	1654	Settlers from Virginia	Rice, tobacco, and pitch, tar from pine trees
South Carolina			
Charles Town	1663	English and other Europeans	Rice, tobacco, pitch, and tar from pine trees.
Georgia			
	1732	James Oglethorpe, who brought English debtors to protect Georgia from the Spanish	Tobacco, indigo

GOVERNMENT	RELIGION
Governor appointed by king	Puritan
Elected by colonists	Complete religious freedom for all — Baptist, Anglican (Episcopalian), and others
Elected by colonists	Several religions, mostly Protestant
Governor appointed by king	Several religions, mostly Protestant
Governor appointed by king	Dutch Reformed, others
Governor appointed by king	Quaker, Dutch Reformed, others
Proprietor selected the governor	Quaker
Proprietor selected the governor	Quaker
Governor appointed by king	Anglican
Proprietor selected the governor	Catholic, Protestant
Governor appointed by king	Several religions, mostly Protestant
Governor appointed by king	Several religions, mostly Protestant
Governor appointed by king	Baptist and other Protestant

5 The French and Indian War (1754-1763)

Causes of the French and Indian War

The French and Indian War was fought by French soldiers together with Native American warriors against British soldiers and American colonists. Although a few tribes sided with the British, most Native Americans were afraid the British would settle on their ancestral lands if they won.

The war lasted until British Major General *James Wolfe* captured Quebec in 1759. This broke the French hold on Canada. When the peace treaty was signed in 1763, France lost most of its territory in North America.

1 In the 1750s, France and Britain were fighting in Europe. Tension between their colonies in the New World also began to increase.

2 The British colonists wanted to take over French lands to make money in the fur trade.

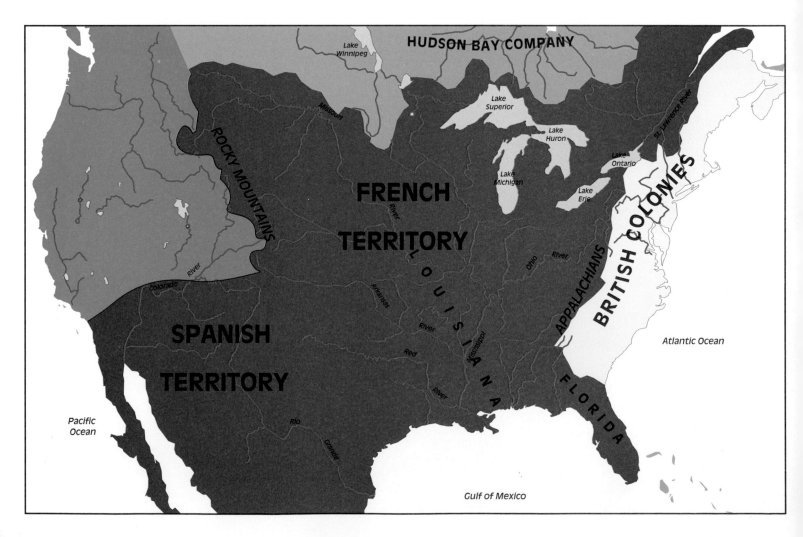

Results of the French and Indian War

1 France lost most of its power in North America.

2 Spain got New Orleans and all French territory west of the Mississippi River.

3 Britain got Canada and all French territory east of the Mississippi, except New Orleans.

4 Britain placed all its colonies under strict control and began taxing them to help pay for the cost of the war.

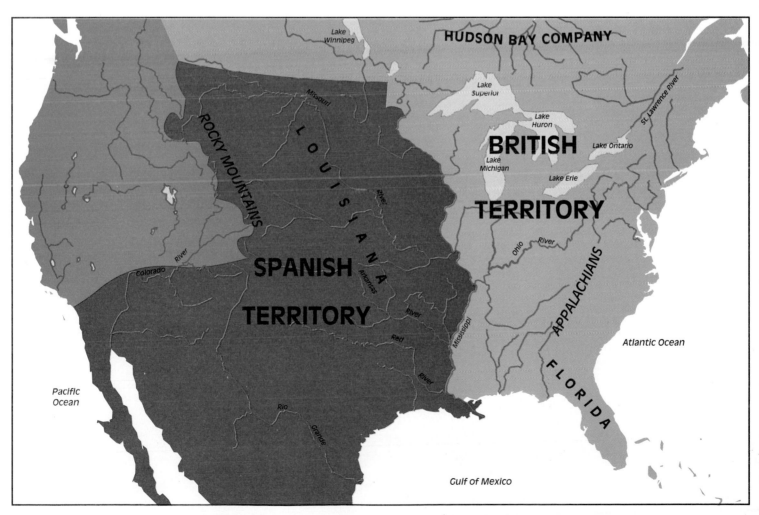

THE AMERICAN REVOLUTION (1775-1783)

1 The Revolution

By 1775, there were serious disagreements between the thirteen British colonies and the British government. No colonists could be elected to the British Parliament in London. Yet, the Parliament passed many taxes that the colonists had to pay. Colonists called this ***taxation without representation***.

The British believed they had every right to tax the colonists. After all, they had paid to defend the colonies in the French and Indian War. Some American colonists did not like the British government to interfere in their lives. The government did not understand colonial life or the hardships brought about by heavy taxation. But, instead of giving the colonists more independence, the British government passed more laws. War broke out. The thirteen colonies successfully revolted against the British, and the United States of America was born.

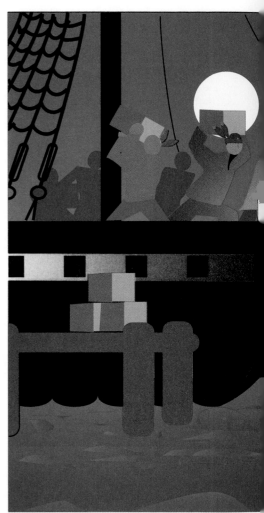

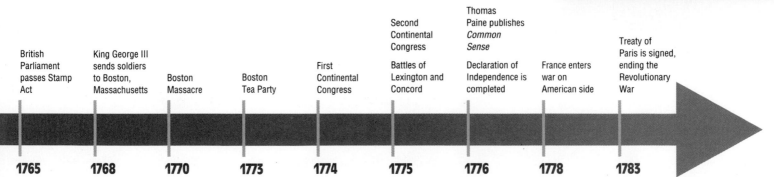

British Parliament passes Stamp Act — 1765

King George III sends soldiers to Boston, Massachusetts — 1768

Boston Massacre — 1770

Boston Tea Party — 1773

First Continental Congress — 1774

Second Continental Congress; Battles of Lexington and Concord — 1775

Thomas Paine publishes *Common Sense*; Declaration of Independence is completed — 1776

France enters war on American side — 1778

Treaty of Paris is signed, ending the Revolutionary War — 1783

Causes of the American Revolution

1 In 1763, Parliament issued the Proclamation of 1763, which ordered colonists not to settle west of the Appalachian Mountains. The British government believed this would keep peace with the Native Americans. The colonists thought the British government should not interfere.

2 In 1765, Parliament passed the Stamp Act. It forced colonists to pay a tax on almost everything printed on paper—newspapers, legal documents—even playing cards. The colonists reacted so strongly against the tax that Parliament revoked it a year later.

3 In 1767, Parliament passed the Townshend Acts, which taxed lead, glass, paper, paint, and tea imported to the colonies. Americans resisted by refusing to buy these items. Finally, the tax was lifted on everything except tea.

4 In 1768, 4,000 British soldiers moved into Boston. Many colonists were forced to keep them in their homes, so Boston became an occupied city. This occupation eventually triggered the Boston Massacre (see pp. 22-23).

5 In 1773, British East India Company ships full of tea were docked in Boston Harbor. On December 16, colonists dressed as Mohawks boarded the ships. They dumped the tea in the water. The event is known today as the Boston Tea Party.

6 To punish the colonists for dumping the tea, the British passed even stricter laws. The colonists called these laws the Intolerable Acts, because the colonists decided they would not tolerate (accept) them (see p. 22).

Boston Tea Party

Results of the American Revolution

1 The thirteen colonies became an independent nation called the United States of America, and was recognized by Britain.

2 Britain gave the United States the land east of the Mississippi River, north to Canada, and south to the border of Florida.

3 All British control of American trade was lifted.

4 A new government with elected representatives was formed under the Articles of Confederation (see p. 28).

5 The successful revolution encouraged other people, especially the French, to overthrow their governments.

The First Continental Congress

The First Continental Congress met to protest the ***Intolerable Acts***. Colonial leaders met in Philadelphia. Every colony except Georgia sent ***delegates***, or representatives. In September 1774, the Congress demanded that the Intolerable Acts be taken back and that the colonists be given more power in making decisions.

The Second Continental Congress

The Second Continental Congress met in Philadelphia in May 1775, a month after the American Revolution had begun. The colonists realized it was important to act together if they were to defeat the British. They agreed to form an American Continental Army. ***John Adams,*** the leader of the Massachusetts delegates, proposed that ***George Washington*** of Virginia become commander-in-chief. Everyone voted for Washington.

minuteman   redcoat

▶ *American casualties: 25,300 dead.*

▶ *"Don't fire until you see the whites of their eyes." These words were spoken by Captain Israel Putnam at the Battle of Bunker Hill, on June 17, 1775.*

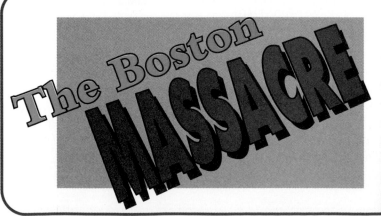

The Boston MASSACRE

2 The Declaration of Independence

The *Continental Congress* appointed a committee to write a document declaring independence for the thirteen colonies. The committee included *Thomas Jefferson*, *Benjamin Franklin*, *John Adams*, *Roger Sherman*, and *Robert Livingston*.

Jefferson, a skilled writer, was the principal author. He talked with his colleagues about the main ideas of the document and completed the Declaration of Independence in three weeks. Jefferson wrote that "all men are created equal, that they are endowed with certain unalienable [unchangeable] rights," including "life, liberty, and the pursuit of happiness." Very few changes were made in the document before it was signed on July 4, 1776—a date remembered today as Independence Day, the first U.S. national holiday.

The Main Points of the Declaration of Independence

1 The nature of a fair government recognizes that people are born with certain rights, including life, liberty, and the pursuit of happiness; and that a government is formed to protect these rights.

2 King George III and the British government behaved unfairly. The Declaration lists many insults, taxes, and other problems the colonists had put up with over the years of British dominion.

3 The colonies intend to form a new nation. Since Britain would not listen to their complaints, the colonists claim their independence and their ability to set up their own government.

In 1768, the city of Boston was occupied by British soldiers. These troops were nicknamed *redcoats* because of the color of their jackets. On March 5, 1770, a number of colonists got in an argument with the redcoats and began throwing snowballs and chunks of ice at them. The soldiers fired shots into the angry but unarmed crowd. Five Americans were killed. The British soldiers were brought to court. *John Adams* defended the soldiers. Two were found guilty of manslaughter and the others were declared innocent. Revolutionaries publicized this story to build support for colonial independence, calling it *The Boston Massacre*.

Some People in the Revolution

Abigail
Adams

Abigail Adams was intelligent, independent-minded, and wrote many long letters about life in colonial Massachusetts. She believed in the equality of the sexes, and wrote to her husband, *John Adams*, as he helped write the Declaration of Independence. Both her husband and her son, *John Quincy Adams*, became President of the United States.

Ethan Allen led Vermont troops called Green Mountain Boys in the American Revolution. When the war broke out, Allen took the Green Mountain Boys to New York to defeat the British at the Battle of Ticonderoga. Next, Allen tried to take Montreal, Canada, but was captured and sent to England as a prisoner of war. He was released at the end of the war.

A former slave who had become a dockworker, *Crispus Attucks* was among those to die in the Boston Massacre and the first African American to give his life for the United States.

Sarah Bache and *Esther Reed* inspired a group of Philadelphia women to go door-to-door to raise money for *George Washington's* troops. They used the money they raised to buy cloth and sew shirts for the soldiers.

One of seventeen children, *Benjamin Franklin* was a writer, printer, inventor, and diplomat. Franklin represented the American colonies in London and later persuaded the French to aid the colonists' cause in the American Revolution. He also invented bifocals, a stove that is named for him, and the lightning rod. He started the first public library, the first fire department, and the first insurance company in North America. Among his writings is *Poor Richard's Almanack*, a collection of proverbs and other wise sayings, such as "A penny saved is a penny earned."

A hero of the American Revolution (see pp. 20-22), *Nathan Hale* attended Yale College before becoming a lieutenant in the Connecticut state army. In the fall of 1776, Hale volunteered for the dangerous mission of spying on the British for General *George Washington*. He was discovered and hanged without a trial. His famous last words were: "I only regret that I have but one life to lose for my country."

A lawyer and great public speaker, *Patrick Henry* became famous when he challenged

many of the British taxes (including the Stamp Act) in court and won. He inspired many people with his speeches, which were filled with such daring statements such as: "Give me liberty or give me death."

An Englishman who came to America to help the colonies, *Thomas Paine* wrote a pamphlet called *Common Sense* in January 1776. His writings helped persuade many colonists that it was only common sense to be independent of Britain and to show the world how people could rule themselves.

Colonists in Massachusetts started putting away military supplies in the town of Concord early in 1775. The British found out and decided to destroy them. But people in Boston discovered the British plans. They sent *Paul Revere*, a famous silversmith, and *William Dawes* on a midnight ride to warn the colonists in Lexington that the British were coming. When the British arrived in Lexington, they were met by seventy *minutemen* (American colonists who agreed to fight at a minute's notice). By the time the British reached Concord, there were thousands of minutemen assembled and ready to fight.

In 1772, a slave named *Phillis Wheatley* wrote a poem about America's struggle for freedom. She compared this struggle with her own desire to be free. She is America's first noted African American poet.

Europeans Who Helped the Americans

Many Europeans came to help the colonists in their fight for independence. France became the colonists' main ally. France sent money and supplies to the colonists and, later, troops. French officers, including the *Marquis de Lafayette* and the *Comte de Rochambeau*, held high positions in the Continental Army. Their military skill helped the colonists win the war, particularly at sea. When the United States signed a treaty with France in 1778, France became the first European nation to recognize the United States as an independent country.

Other Europeans were inspired by the ideals of the American Revolution and came to fight on the side of the colonists. *Baron Friedrich von Steuben*, who drilled Washington's troops, came from Prussia. *Thaddeus Kosciusko*, a brilliant army engineer, came from Poland. *Casimir Pulaski*, also from Poland, rose to the rank of Brigadier General and Chief of Cavalry. He was killed leading a cavalry charge in an attack on Savannah, Georgia.

While Americans were given this support freely, the British had to hire troops from Germany called *Hessians* to help them. Nearly 30,000 Hessians fought for the British in the Revolutionary War.

Thaddeus Kosciusko

Marquis de Lafayette

"I have not yet begun to fight." These words were spoken by John Paul Jones of the U.S. Navy, September 23, 1779.

America's Most Famous Traitor

Benedict Arnold was a brave American soldier, but he felt that his service to the colonies had not been rewarded enough. He was also angry that the *Continental Congress* had investigated some of his questionable business deals. So, when offered money by the British in return for secret information, Arnold accepted and helped the British in a plot to capture the fort at West Point, New York.

On the night of September 23, 1780, three Revolutionary soldiers captured a young British major, *John André*. André was disguised as a civilian, but he was carrying papers that showed Arnold's plot. Arnold, in command of the fort at West Point, was going to turn the fort over to the British. The fall of West Point would open up the entire Hudson Valley to the British!

Benedict Arnold escaped to a British warship in the Hudson River. He was made an officer in the British Army. Arnold was well paid for his treason—6,315 British pounds plus an annual pension of 500 pounds. André was convicted by the Americans and hanged as a spy.

Chronology of the American Revolution

1775

April 19	The war begins when fighting breaks out at Lexington and Concord, Massachusetts
May 10	Second Continental Congress opens in Philadelphia, Penn. Americans capture Fort Ticonderoga, New York
June 15	George Washington named Commander-in-Chief
June 17	Battle of Bunker Hill, Boston, Massachusetts
December	Battle of Quebec, Canada

1776

March 17	British leave Boston, Massachusetts
July 4	Declaration of Independence signed
August 27	Battle of Long Island, New York
September 15	British occupy New York City
November 16	British capture Fort Washington, New York
November 20	British capture Fort Lee, New Jersey
December 26	Battle of Trenton, New Jersey

1777

January 3	Battle of Princeton, New Jersey
July 6	British capture Fort Ticonderoga, New York
September 11	Battle of Brandywine, Pennsylvania
September 19	First Battle of Freeman's Farm (Saratoga), New York
September 26	British capture Philadelphia, Pennsylvania
October 4	Battle of Germantown, Pennsylvania
October 7	Americans win Second Battle of Freeman's Farm, New York
October 17	British General John Burgoyne surrenders at Saratoga, New York
December 19	Washington moves his army to Valley Forge, Pennsylvania

1778

February 6	Americans sign treaty with France
June 28	Battle of Monmouth, New Jersey
December 29	British occupy Savannah, Georgia

1779

June 21	Spain declares war on Britain
September 23	John Paul Jones captures the British frigate Serapis

1780

May 12	Americans under Benjamin Lincoln surrender at Charleston, South Carolina
August 16	Battle of Camden, South Carolina
October 7	Battle of Kings Mountain, North and South Carolina

1781

March 15	Battle of Guilford Court House, North Carolina
September 28	Battle of Yorktown, Virginia, begins
October 19	British General Charles Cornwallis surrenders at Yorktown, Pennsylvania

1782

July 11	British leave Savannah, Georgia
November 30	Draft of peace treaty signed in Paris, France
December 14	British leave Charleston, South Carolina

1783

April 15	United States ratifies peace treaty draft
September 3	Final peace treaty signed in Paris (called the Treaty of Paris)

THE BIRTH OF A NEW NATION (1783-1800)

1 The Articles of Confederation

The first American government was called a ***confederation***. It consisted of all thirteen states. The Continental Congress (see p. 22) sent delegates to the government, and each state had one vote. For major laws to be passed, nine of the thirteen states had to agree. There was no king or president. The confederation lasted for eight years, from 1781 to 1789. It was an unusual government for its time because it had a written constitution and no monarch. The constitution of the Confederation was called the ***Articles of Confederation***. It provided for a central government that was weaker than the state governments.

The Liberty Bell, which hangs in Independence Hall in Philadelphia, Pennsylvania, bears an inscription from Leviticus XXV,10: "Proclaim liberty throughout all the land unto all the inhabitants thereof."

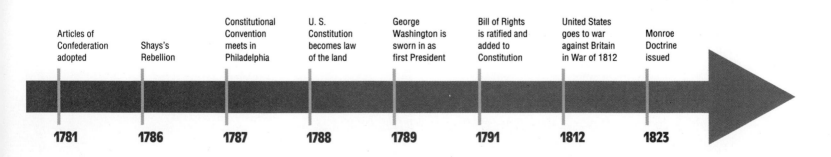

1781	1786	1787	1788	1789	1791	1812	1823
Articles of Confederation adopted	Shays's Rebellion	Constitutional Convention meets in Philadelphia	U. S. Constitution becomes law of the land	George Washington is sworn in as first President	Bill of Rights is ratified and added to Constitution	United States goes to war against Britain in War of 1812	Monroe Doctrine issued

Powers of the National Government Under the Confederation

1 To declare war and make peace

2 To coin and borrow money

3 To deal with foreign countries and sign treaties

4 To operate post offices

Weaknesses of the Articles of Confederation

1 The national government could not force the states to obey its laws.

2 It did not have the power to tax.

3 It did not have the power to enforce the laws.

4 Congress lacked strong and steady leadership.

5 There was no national army or navy.

6 There was no national system of courts.

7 Each state could issue its own paper money.

8 Each state could put tariffs on trade between states. (A tariff is a tax on goods coming in from another state or country.)

Shays's Rebellion

In 1786, the American economy was in trouble. Many people could not pay their debts. Some lost their property. Some went to jail as debtors. The price farmers could get for their crops dropped.

Farmers in Massachusetts started an armed rebellion against the state. Their leader was **Daniel Shays**, a Revolutionary War captain. He asked the Massachusetts government to ease up on debtors. When it did not, his troops conducted raids all over the state. Since there was no national army, the Massachusetts state government had to put down the rebellion alone. Shays's Rebellion showed the leaders of the new states that they needed a stronger national government than was provided for by the Articles of Confederation.

2 The Constitution of the United States

The Constitutional Convention

In May 1787, fifty-five delegates from every state except Rhode Island met in Philadelphia. *George Washington* served as president of the convention. *James Madison* took detailed notes of the meetings. The delegates at the convention decided to write a new constitution. Four months later, the document was completed.

The constitution they created is now the highest law of the United States. It provides for citizens to elect the officials who govern them. It establishes that power is shared between the national government and the state governments. In the national, or *federal*, government, there is a *legislative branch* (Congress), which makes the laws, an *executive branch* headed by the President which carries out the laws, and a *judicial branch* headed by the Supreme Court, which decides if the laws are *constitutional*, or applied correctly. The power of each branch can be controlled by the other two. This is called the system of *checks and balances* (see p. 114).

The Constitution of the United States was signed on September 17, 1787. In order for it to become the law of the land, it had to be *ratified* (approved) by at least nine of the thirteen states. By the summer of 1788, all the states except North Carolina and Rhode Island had voted for ratification. These two states ratified the Constitution after the government was already operating.

On September 17, 1787, the U.S. Constitution was adopted in Congress at Independence Hall, Philadelphia, Pennsylvania.

▶ *In 1803, an event occurred that showed that our system of checks and balances really works. In a case known as* **Marbury v. Madison,** *the Supreme Court declared that a section of the Judiciary Act of 1789 was unconstitutional (contrary to the meaning of the Constitution). This case showed that the judicial branch had the power to check laws passed by the executive branch.*

The Bill of Rights

Even though the Constitution was ratified, many people feared the central government would have too much power. The Bill of Rights was added to the Constitution after opponents of the Constitution convinced the nation that a strong central government without safeguards for the people was a danger to liberty.

The Bill of Rights consists of ten amendments, or additions, to the Constitution. It guarantees basic liberties, such as freedom of speech, of the press, and of religion. It was ratified in 1791, three years after the Constitution went into effect (see Amendments to the Constitution, p. 120).

3 Formation of a New Government

The first Presidential election under the Constitution was held on January 7, 1789. *George Washington* was elected President, and *John Adams,* Vice President. None of the Presidential electors voted against Washington. The government first met in New York in March 1789, and Washington was *inaugurated* (sworn into office) on April 30.

First Acts of the New Government

1 Congress passed the Judiciary Act of 1789. This law said that the Supreme Court would have six judges. Washington appointed John Jay as the first Chief Justice.

2 Congress approved the Bill of Rights and sent it to the states for ratification.

3 The President formed the first cabinet, the group of leaders appointed to help him run the government.

The **Democratic-Republican** *and the* **Federalist** *parties were the first major political parties in the United States. In 1824, Andrew Jackson renamed his branch of the Democratic-Republicans* **Democrats** — *the same party we know today. After the War of 1812 (see p. 35) the Federalist party was in disarray. The new opposition to the Democrats were the* **Whigs.** *Later, in the 1850s, the Whigs joined up with the* **Free Soil Party,** *later known as the* **Republican** *party. Abraham Lincoln became the first Republican President (see p. 58).*

George Washington's Cabinet

Secretary of War	Henry Knox (Massachusetts)
Secretary of the Treasury	Alexander Hamilton (New York)
Secretary of State	Thomas Jefferson (Virginia)
Attorney General	Edmund Randolph (Virginia)

The Beginning of Political Parties

George Washington did not want the United States to have political parties, but, during his second term in office, people started to form them anyway. Two major parties emerged. The country's second president, *John Adams,* was a Federalist. He was defeated in 1800 by *Thomas Jefferson*, a Democratic-Republican. When Jefferson was inaugurated as President, power passed peacefully from one political party to another. This was important evidence that, in the United States, the democratic process worked.

Benjamin Banneker was an African-American inventor who studied mathematics, astronomy, and mechanics. In 1790, he was appointed by President *George Washington* to help measure and lay out the city of Washington, D.C.

The Reverend *Absalom Jones* was a free African American who became a distinguished leader in Philadelphia. He founded the *Free African Society*, a civic organization. During the War of 1812 (see p. 34), he recruited 2,500 free African Americans to help defend Philadelphia.

Francis Scott Key was a young lawyer who wrote the poem, *The Star Spangled Banner*, after being inspired by watching the Americans fight off the British attack of Baltimore during the War of 1812 (see p. 34). The poem became the words to the national anthem.

Dolley Madison was the wife of President *James Madison* and was First Lady during the War of 1812 (see p. 34). While the British were burning Washington, D.C., she stayed behind to pack up important presidential papers, the White House silverware, and a famous portrait of *George Washington*, painted by American artist *Gilbert Stuart*. Her courage kept these items from falling into British hands.

Mercy Otis Warren received a college education by studying her brother's notes from Dartmouth College. During the American Revolution (see pp. 20-22), she wrote plays, poems, and articles that made fun of the British and helped raise the spirits of Americans. In 1805, she published a three-volume history of the American Revolution.

Eli Whitney invented the cotton gin in 1793. This machine, which picked the seeds from cotton, made the production of cotton much more profitable. It also encouraged a rise in the slave trade to Southern states, where plantation owners could process more cotton with more slaves to farm it.

Francis Scott Key

Dolley Madison

4 The War of 1812

The American Revolution (see pp. 20-22) gave Americans independence. The *War of 1812* guaranteed that other nations of the world would treat the United States with respect.

"Don't give up the ship!" These words were spoken on June 1, 1813, by U.S. Navy Captain James Lawrence.

Causes of the War of 1812

1 Great Britain and France were taking U.S. ships. This interfered with American trade.

2 The United States made a deal with France: the United States would stop trading with Britain if the French would stop taking U.S. ships.

3 The United States thought the British were arming Native Americans to attack settlers in the Northwest Territory, the land north of the Ohio River between the organized states and the Mississippi River.

4 The United States thought that Britain was still interfering with its former colonies.

5 The United States wanted to take Canada from Britain and Florida from Spain.

A superior British navy was not enough to defeat a spirited young nation.

Events of the War of 1812

1 The United States tried to invade Canada several times but never succeeded.

2 British plans to invade the United States from Canada were stopped by Captain Oliver Perry on Lake Erie and Captain Thomas Macdonough on Lake Champlain. Perry reported his victory with his famous line, "We have met the enemy and they are ours."

3 Early in the war, the ships U.S.S. Constitution and U.S.S.United States won great victories and became famous throughout the country. The British eventually gained control of the seas.

4 The British captured and burned Washington, D.C., and then bombed Fort McHenry in Baltimore, Maryland.

5 Although the peace treaty was signed in Paris in December 1814, news didn't arrive in the United States fast enough to stop a British attempt to invade New Orleans in January 1815. Commander Andrew Jackson defeated the invasion, however, and became a national hero.

Results of the War of 1812

1 The British recognized U.S. boundaries and stayed out of the Northwest Territory.

2 The United States gained national pride from its victories at sea and at New Orleans.

3 American industry prospered because it made more goods at home when trade stopped with Britain.

4 The Federalist Party, which had been the party of John Adams and Alexander Hamilton, disappeared. Federalists had opposed the war.

"We have met the enemy and they are ours." These words were sent by Commodore Oliver Hazard Perry to General William H. Harrison after the U.S. victory of The Battle of Lake Erie, September 10, 1813.

5 The Monroe Doctrine

The United States emerged with confidence from the War of 1812 (see pp. 34-35). This confidence was expressed in the *Monroe Doctrine* of 1823, issued by the fifth president, *James Monroe*. (A *doctrine* is a principle or policy.) It was one of the nation's first major foreign policy statements. Written by then Secretary of State *John Quincy Adams*, it warned European nations not to try to establish new colonies in the Americas.

At the time the Monroe Doctrine was issued, U.S. leaders were afraid Spain might try to recapture its lost colonies in South America. The South American countries of Colombia and Argentina had recently overthrown their Spanish governments, and were setting an example of self-rule for other colonies.

James Monroe

The Main Points of the Monroe Doctrine

1 European countries could no longer form colonies in North or South America.

2 The political systems of the Americas were separate from those of Europe.

3 The United States would consider any attempt by Europe to influence politics in the Americas as a threat to its "peace and safety."

4 The United States would not interfere in European governments or their existing colonies.

The years following the War of 1812 were years of expansion and growth for the United States. President Monroe wanted to preserve the right to grow for the United States, which inspired his message to European nations in the Monroe Doctrine.

WESTWARD HO! THE EXPANSION WEST (1800-1900)

WESTWARD HO! THE EXPANSION WEST (1800-1900)

1 The Louisiana Purchase

In 1803, the United States bought the Louisiana Territory from the French Emperor **Napoleon**. The territory had been named for **King Louis XIV** of France. Its boundaries stretched from New Orleans, up the Mississippi River, and west to the Rocky Mountains. President **Thomas Jefferson**'s Secretary of State, **James Madison,** paid fifteen million dollars for 828,000 square miles, or about three cents an acre, to make the **Louisiana Purchase**.

As settlers from the United States moved into the Louisiana Territory, there were bitter wars between them and the Native Americans, whose ancestors had lived on these lands for centuries. Few settlers thought they needed to buy the land from the Native Americans, since the United States had already bought it from the French. Eventually most tribes were forced off the lands.

BRITISH TERRITORY

Missouri River

River

Ohio River

Arkansas River

Mississippi

Red River

New Orleans

- United States before 1803
- Louisiana Purchase
- Spanish Territory
- Territory disputed among Russia, Spain, Great Britain, and the United States

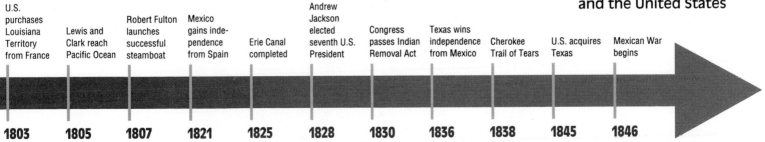

1803	1805	1807	1821	1825	1828	1830	1836	1838	1845	1846
U.S. purchases Louisiana Territory from France	Lewis and Clark reach Pacific Ocean	Robert Fulton launches successful steamboat	Mexico gains independence from Spain	Erie Canal completed	Andrew Jackson elected seventh U.S. President	Congress passes Indian Removal Act	Texas wins independence from Mexico	Cherokee Trail of Tears	U.S. acquires Texas	Mexican War begins

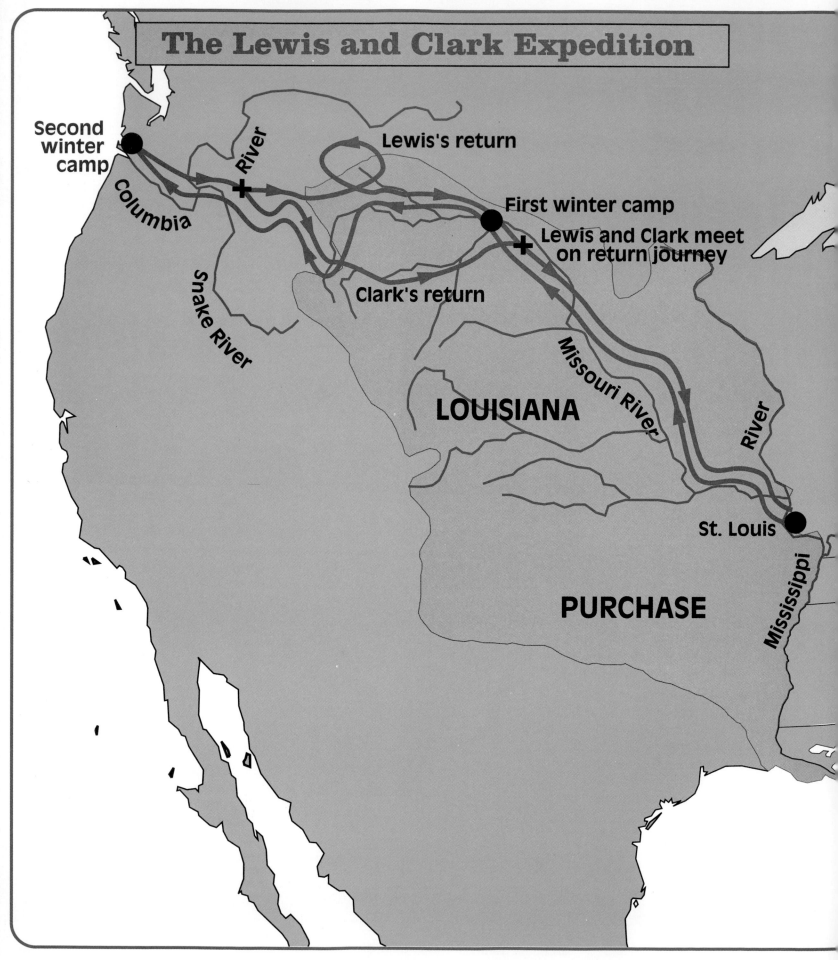

The Lewis and Clark Expedition

Second winter camp

Lewis's return

First winter camp

Lewis and Clark meet on return journey

Columbia

River

Snake River

Clark's return

Missouri River

LOUISIANA

River

St. Louis

PURCHASE

Mississippi

OHIO River

President *Thomas Jefferson* sent *Meriwether Lewis* and *William Clark*, officers in the United States Army and experienced frontiersmen, on an expedition to learn more about the lands in the Louisiana Territory.

An All-Water Route to the Pacific

The purpose of the Lewis and Clark expedition was to follow the Missouri River to its source and to find an all-water route to the Pacific Ocean. The explorers also planned to collect information about plants, animals, climate, and geographical features along the way.

Help on the Expedition

Lewis, Clark, and about thirty other men started their journey in St. Louis, Missouri, in 1804. They traveled along the Missouri River to an area near present day Bismarck, North Dakota. Here they built Fort Mandan and spent the winter. When spring arrived, the explorers continued to travel up the Missouri River.

Lewis and Clark had a French-Canadian guide who was married to a Native American woman of the Shoshone tribe. Her name was *Sacajewea*. She helped lead the expedition to the Shoshone, who welcomed them and gave them horses, supplies, guides, and advice on how to travel over the Rocky Mountains on ancient trails.

On the other side of the Rockies, the explorers set up camp on Nez Perce Indian lands. The Nez Perce gave the explorers food and shelter as they recovered from the difficult trip. Then the explorers built canoes to travel by river to the Pacific Ocean.

A Successful Expedition

On November 15, 1805, the explorers reached the Pacific Ocean. They built Fort Clatsop and waited out the winter. In March 1806, they started home, arriving in St. Louis seven months later.

The entire expedition took twenty-eight months and covered 7,500 miles. It encouraged exploration and white settlement of the Western territories and led to the end of a way of life for the many Native Americans who lived there.

2 Routes of Expansion

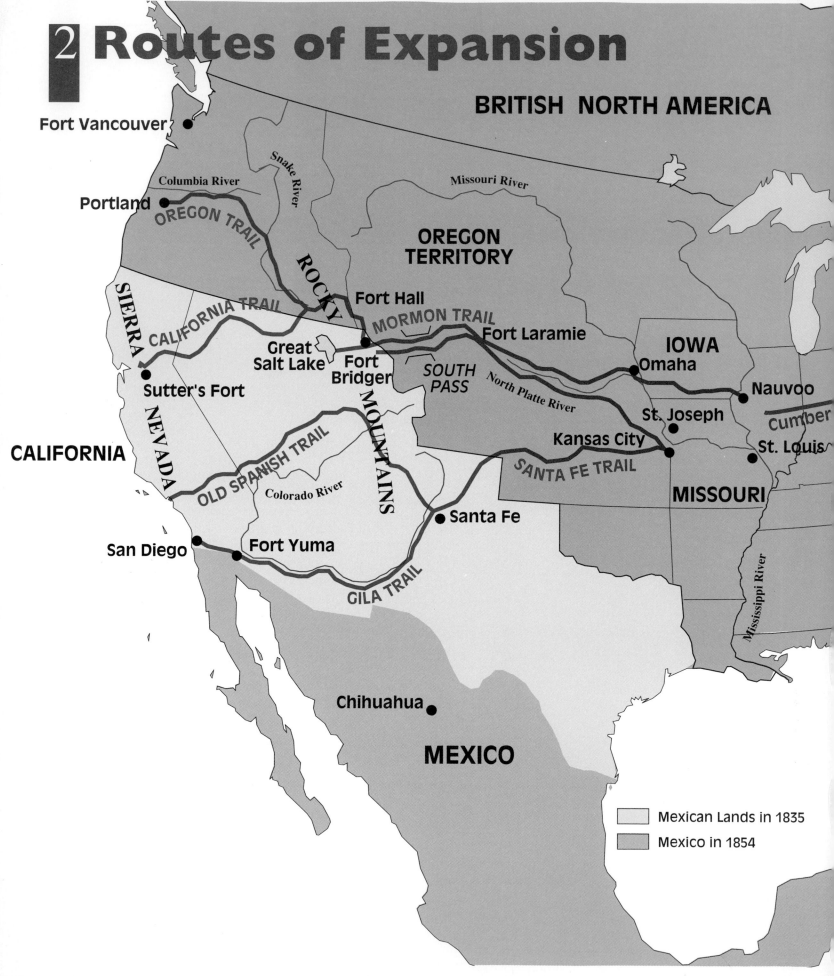

BRITISH NORTH AMERICA

Fort Vancouver

Snake River

Columbia River

Missouri River

Portland

OREGON TRAIL

ROCKY

OREGON TERRITORY

Fort Hall

MORMON TRAIL

Fort Laramie

SIERRA

CALIFORNIA TRAIL

IOWA

Great Salt Lake

Fort Bridger

SOUTH PASS

Omaha

North Platte River

NEVADA

Sutter's Fort

MOUNTAINS

Nauvoo

St. Joseph

Cumber

CALIFORNIA

OLD SPANISH TRAIL

Kansas City

St. Louis

Colorado River

SANTA FE TRAIL

San Diego

Fort Yuma

Santa Fe

MISSOURI

GILA TRAIL

Mississippi River

Chihuahua

MEXICO

Mexican Lands in 1835

Mexico in 1854

THE WESTWARD MOVEMENT

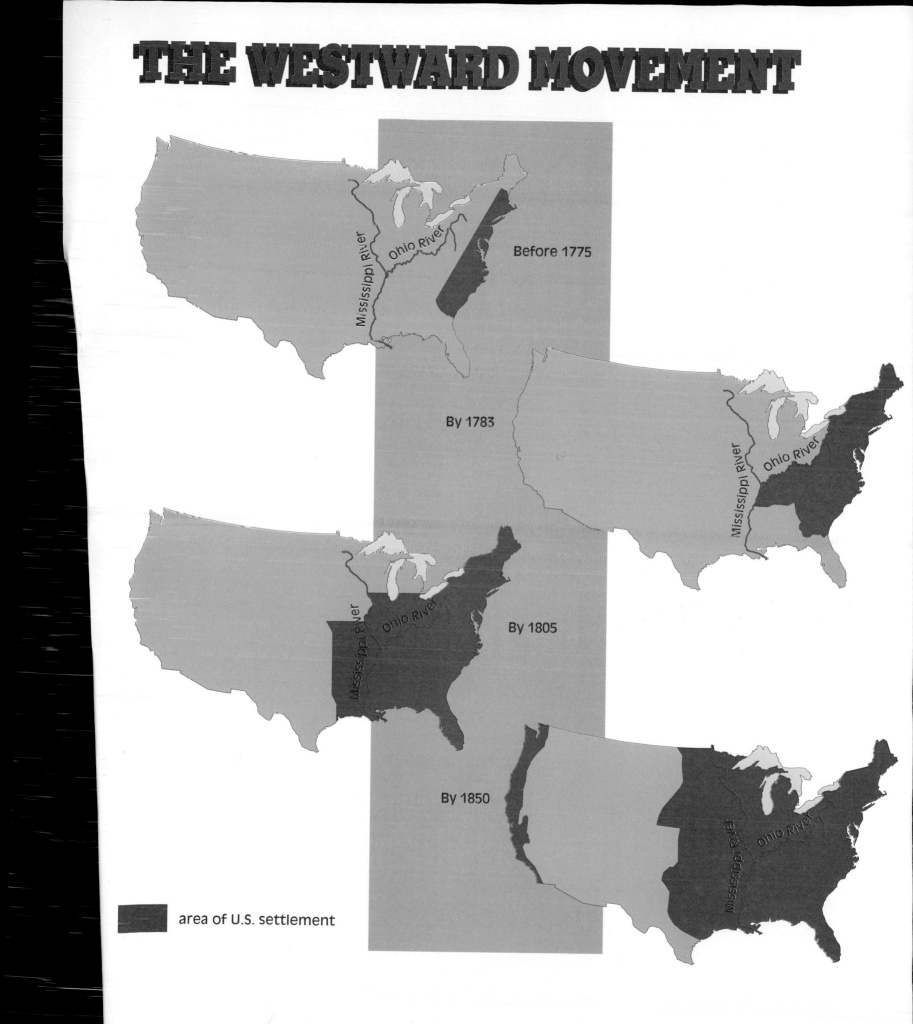

Before 1775

By 1783

By 1805

By 1850

Mississippi River

Ohio River

area of U.S. settlement

By 1800, more and more people were moving west and settling lands long held by Native Americans. Most settlers traveled the rough trails on horseback or in wagons. In some places, canals were built to connect rivers and lakes to make transportation easier and faster. Later, in the 1850s to the 1870s, railroads were built and a whole new age of transportation was begun. By 1900, the U.S. *frontier*—the boundary dividing settled lands and wilderness—had virtually disappeared into the Pacific Ocean.

Overland Routes

Early trails in the U.S. frontier were made by Native Americans and later by fur trappers and traders, who chopped down trees and shrubs to clear rough roadways. As trails became more widely traveled, they were used by wagons. Some trails, called *turnpike roads*, were wagon roads built by private companies that charged fees for their use.

Cumberland Road

In 1811, construction began on a road that would cut across the Allegheny Mountains. This road eventually ran from Cumberland, Maryland, to Vandalia, Illinois.

Oregon Trail

In 1812, **Robert Stuart** crossed the continent from east to west using a route that became known as the **Oregon Trail**. It was 2,000 miles long and took about five months to travel by covered wagon. The trail started at Independence, Missouri, and went to Oregon by way of Soda Springs, Idaho (see California Trail). In the 1840s, thousands of people used this trail.

Santa Fe Trail

The Santa Fe Trail ran from Independence, Missouri, to Santa Fe, New Mexico. It was nearly 800 miles long and passed through the Cimarron Desert. **William Becknell**, a Santa Fe trader, blazed the trail by slashing trees along the way.

Old Spanish Trail

Mexican trader **Antonio Armijo** created a route that carried travelers nearly 900 miles from Santa Fe, New Mexico, to Los Angeles, California. The Gila Trail branched off the Santa Fe Trail at Santa Fe a led to San Diego, California.

California Trail

This trail from Soda Springs, Idaho, to San Francisco, California, branched off the Oregon Trail (see above) slightly north of the Great Lake. Wagons traveling to California turned off the Oregon Trail at S Springs and headed down the California Trail.

Ohio River

Road

42

Means of Transportation

Wagon Trains

Most families moving west to settle new lands for the United States traveled in covered wagons. Some were made from farm wagons, but heavier wagons, called *Conestoga wagons,* were much sturdier and broke down less often when traveling over great distances. Because of their large white canvas tops, these wagons looked like sailboats and were called *prairie schooners* (a schooner is a sailing ship).

The covered wagon was home for pioneers on their journeys. They packed as much as they could into it—farming tools, cooking utensils, food, bedding, weapons, and furniture. The wagon was usually pulled by oxen or mules.

A family wanting to move west joined up with other families to form traveling companies, or *wagon trains*. Companies—sometimes thirty to seventy or more wagons—were formed for safety. A company captain was the leader and the guide. He was often a fur trapper who had been west before.

On their way west, pioneers had to cross many miles of land called the *Great Desert*—so named because there were no trees. Today we call this land the *Great Plains*. If the settlers were going to Oregon or California, they had to cross the Rocky Mountains before winter, when heavy snows blocked the mountain passes. Blistering heat, tornadoes, and dust storms were also among the hardships. Pioneers always risked attack by armed bandits or hostile Native Americans. Many of the pioneers never reached their destinations. Some died, others turned back. Those who made it faced new challenges as they tried to build a life in the West.

 "Go west, young man." *These words were written by John B.L. Soule, in an article in the* **Terre Haute (Indiana) Express,** *1851.*

Pioneers heading west favored Conestoga wagons because they were sturdier than farm wagons. These prairie schooners were usually pulled by oxen or mules in traveling companies called wagon trains.

The Pioneer's Life

Once a pioneer family settled on a piece of land, they built a house. Many pioneers lived in hillside dugouts until a new house could be built. On the prairies where there were few trees, houses were made with sod or earth. The sod was cut into blocks and used like bricks. Where trees were plentiful, as in the Northwest, log cabins were common.

Pioneers had to grow their own food. The whole family helped. Men plowed fields and did other heavy work. Women tended vegetable gardens, made clothes, cooked, and cleaned the house. Children milked cows, fed animals, and collected chickens' eggs.

Pioneer families were often lonely. The nearest neighbor might be twenty or thirty miles away, and the nearest town equally far. Schools were also few and far between, and often were one-room structures where all grades were taught by one teacher.

Although life meant mostly hard work, pioneers did enjoy some opportunities to play. Weddings, barn raisings, births, and holidays were times reserved for fiddlers, dancing, and amusements. The Fourth of July was a favorite holiday celebrated widely throughout the West.

The Stagecoach

Passenger coaches were a popular form of public transportation in the early 1800s. Because the coach driver changed horses every fifteen miles—or *stage*—these horse-pulled coaches were called *stagecoaches*.

Stagecoaches carried people and mail between towns often hundreds of miles apart. Most stagecoaches were very uncomfortable. The passenger cabin was small and held up to nine people. Passengers sat on benches with no backs to lean on. Roads were poor; there was always the chance that the coach driver might drive too fast and tip the coach over.

In addition to the discomfort, travelers faced danger of attack. Outlaws held up coaches for the mail and the money that might be inside, as well as the passengers' possessions. Hostile Native Americans also proved a threat.

In the 1800s, stagecoaches were a popular means of transportation in the West.

44

The Pony Express

The Pony Express delivered mail between St. Joseph, Missouri, and Sacramento, California, in 1860 and 1861. Young men between the ages of fifteen and twenty-five rode horses at top speed, stopping only to change horses, eat, and sleep. Riders changed horses at 153 stations, spaced seven to twenty miles apart. Most riders covered about 250 miles a day. The Pony Express took eight to ten days to deliver the mail almost 2,000 miles. The bravery of the riders made the Pony Express famous, but after only eighteen months it went bankrupt. The service cost more to run than could be charged to customers. The transcontinental telegraph helped put an end to the Pony Express.

REMEMBER THE ALAMO

In 1821, Mexico gained independence from Spain. By 1830, 20,000 Americans had moved into Texas. To raise money, the Mexican government offered land in its Texas Territory for sale at cheap prices. In return for the land, settlers were supposed to learn Spanish and make Roman Catholicism their religion. Many settlers failed to keep up their end of the bargain and, by 1830, immigration from the United States was banned. In 1835, Texas settlers set up their own government. *Sam Houston*, a European-American who had been adopted by the Cherokees, was their leader.

When the Mexican dictator *Antonio Lopez de Santa Anna* tried to put down the Texas government, he found that the settlers had taken over the *Alamo*, a Spanish mission built by Catholic priests near San Antonio. The settlers had set it up as a fort and supply house for guns and ammunition.

Twenty-seven-year-old Colonel *William Travis* was in command of the Alamo. He had only 189 men, including *Davy Crockett*, a former Tennessee Congressman, and *Jim Bowie*, an expert in using knives. Santa Anna brought 4,000 Mexican troops to capture the fort.

For days, the Mexicans attacked the Alamo with gunfire and cannons. Early on Sunday morning, March 6, 1836, Santa Anna ordered his bugler to play a song called *Deguello*, Spanish for "to slit the throat." This was a signal that no one in the Alamo was to be spared. Within an hour and a half, all the fighters inside, as well as 600 Mexicans, were dead.

"Remember the Alamo," a slogan ascribed to Colonel Sidney Sherman on April 21, 1836, became the battle cry for Texas independence. On April 21, 1836, Sam Houston's army caught Santa Anna and made him sign a treaty recognizing Texas's independence. For ten years it was called the Lone Star Republic and, in 1845, Congress voted to make it a U.S. territory. This sparked the **Mexican War** (see p. 48).

Canals

Canals are waterways built to connect large bodies of water. *Locks,* which are sections of canals with water-tight gates at each end, make it possible for boats to travel over different heights of terrain. The gates let a boat in and allow it to move to the next higher or the next lower section of water.

In the early 1800s, many canals were built in Pennsylvania, New Jersey, New York, and elsewhere between the Atlantic Ocean and the Mississippi River. By joining eastern rivers to the Great Lakes and the rivers of the West, the canals eased travel and greatly lowered the cost of shipping goods to markets on the east coast. Horses walking along a towpath pulled passenger boats. Mules pulled freight barges. Canal travel was more comfortable, safer, and faster than the trip by wagon or stagecoach (see pp. 43-44).

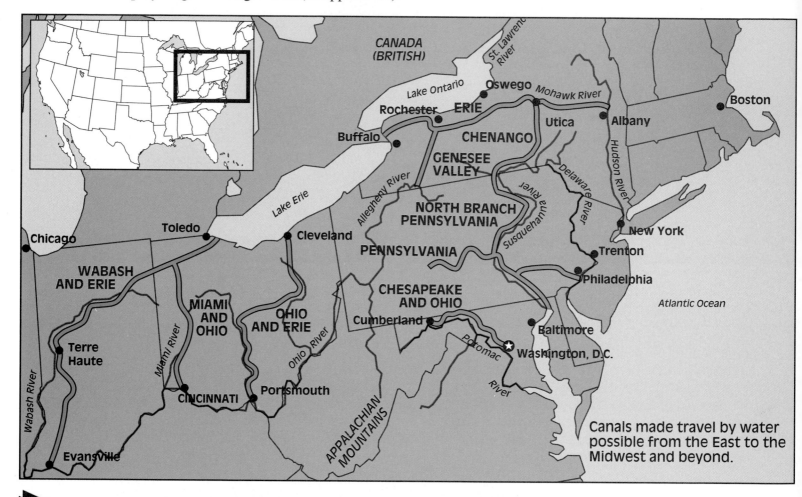

Canals made travel by water possible from the East to the Midwest and beyond.

> *The Erie Canal brought more shipping business through New York Harbor than any other Eastern port. The canal helped make New York City the largest city in the United States.*

Dewitt Clinton, governor of New York, persuaded the state to build a major canal from the Hudson River to Lake Erie to provide an easier route than the rough roads across the Allegheny Mountains. The *Erie Canal* was started in 1817 and finished in 1825. It was 360 miles long–only the Grand Canal of China was longer. It made it possible to travel by boat from the Great Lakes to the Atlantic Ocean. The Erie Canal shortened the trip from Buffalo to Albany, New York, from three weeks to one.

Railroads

The first locomotive built in the United States, called *The Best Friend of Charleston*, went into service on December 25, 1830. At about the same time, a New Yorker named *Peter Cooper* designed a small steam locomotive. He named it the *Tom Thumb* after a tiny storybook character. It ran on thirteen miles of track. The Tom Thumb convinced people that the "iron horse," as the locomotive was called, would soon replace the real horse. Thousands of miles of railroads were built in the 1850s and 1860s. Trains carried passengers and freight westward to the banks of the Missouri River. Soon railroads became the favored means of transportation.

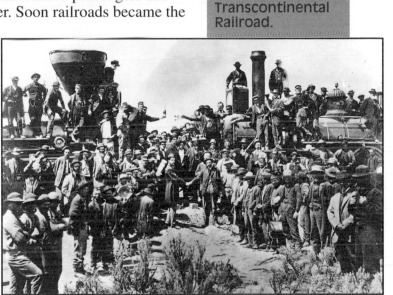

On July 1, 1862, President *Abraham Lincoln* signed the Pacific Railroad Act, which called for building a railroad from Omaha, Nebraska, to Sacramento, California. The laying of 1,500 miles of track began at both ends in 1863. The Union Pacific laid westbound track out of Omaha with a team of Irish immigrants, African Americans, and Civil War veterans. The tracks of the Central Pacific were laid eastbound from Sacramento by 5,000 laborers, most of whom had been recruited in China by the railroad. The two tracks met in Promontory, Utah, on May 10, 1869. The completion of the *Transcontinental Railroad* made it possible to travel by train all the way from the east coast to Sacramento, California.

The Central Pacific and the Union Pacific meet up in Promontory, Utah, to complete the Transcontinental Railroad.

Trains traveled the Transcontinental Railroad at about twenty-five miles per hour. It took ten to twelve days to go from Omaha to Sacramento. Original fares were forty dollars for a bench seat or one hundred dollars for a luxurious sleeper car.

The iron horse was the favored means of transportation in the United States by the late 1800s.

③ The Mexican War (1846-1848)

Causes of the Mexican War

1 Mexico was opposed to Texas becoming a U.S. territory.

2 The United States claimed that the southern boundary of Texas was the Rio Grande River. Mexico claimed it was the Nueces River, further north.

3 President Polk used this border dispute to justify moving U.S. troops into Mexican territory.

James Knox Polk

After Texas won independence in 1836, Mexico continued to claim much of its land and refused to recognize the Rio Grande River as its boundary. When Texas became a U.S. territory in 1845, the United States hoped that Mexico would turn over much of its other territory. This included parts of present-day New Mexico, Arizona, Nevada, Utah, and California. President **James Polk** believed that the United States had a right to this land. Polk believed in the doctrine of **Manifest Destiny**, the idea that it was the will of God for the United States to extend from the Atlantic to the Pacific.

Mexico refused to sell the land and instead cut its ties with the United States. In May 1846, the United States declared war on Mexico. The U.S. army was too strong for the Mexicans led by **Antonio Lopez de Santa Anna**. General **Zachary Taylor** won many victories in northern Mexico. General **Winfield Scott** captured Mexico City, Mexico's capital. Captain **John C. Fremont** drove the Mexicans out of California. The United States won the war easily.

Results of the Mexican War

1 Mexico agreed that the Rio Grande River was the southern boundary of Texas.

2 Mexico gave all of present-day California, Nevada, and Utah, as well as parts of Arizona, New Mexico, Colorado, and Wyoming to the United States. The United States paid Mexico $15 million for this land, called the Mexican Cession.

3 The size and influence of the United States increased once again.

The Gadsden Purchase

In 1853, five years after the Mexican War, the United States paid Mexico ten million dollars for another strip of land in southern New Mexico and Arizona. U.S. Railroad companies wanted to build train routes to California on this land. This transaction was called the Gadsden Purchase after *James Gadsden*, the ambassador to Mexico who negotiated the purchase.

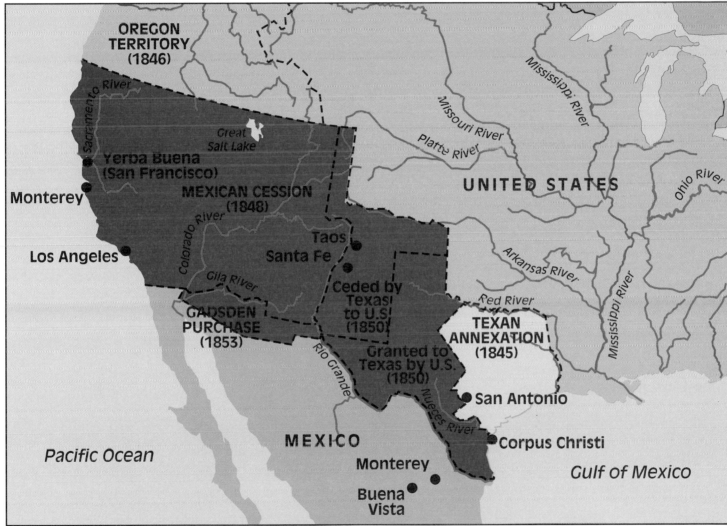

Lands acquired by the United States in the Mexican Cession, Texan Annexation, and Gadsden Purchase

Gold Rush

There's Gold in Them Thar Hills

On January 24, 1848, one week before the Mexican War ended (see p. 48), *James Marshall* made a discovery. Marshall worked for *John Sutter*, who had founded a fort at present-day Sacramento, California. While clearing out the stream that carried water to Sutter's sawmill, Marshall turned up some glittering yellow flakes. The flakes were gold, and there was plenty of it in the surrounding hills.

It took about a year for news that gold had been found to reach the east coast. But when the word arrived, thousands of people moved to California in what became known as the *Gold Rush*. Those who arrived were called *forty-niners*, because 1849 was the height of the rush. In the hopes of getting rich, forty-niners risked getting robbed or killed. There was little law and order to protect them in the mining towns. Yet very few found enough gold to become rich.

Mining Gold

In order to find gold in a stream, some miners panned for the precious metal. They used a shallow pan to scoop up water and rocks. After sifting through the pans and slowly removing the water, they sometimes found gold, which is heavier than many other rocks. Other forty-niners dug in the soil or cleared rock to mine gold ore.

By 1850, nearly all the gold around Sutter's Mill was gone. People were lucky to find more than ten dollars' worth. But people kept coming to California. Its population grew from about 14,000 in 1848 to 225,000 in 1852.

panning for gold

4 The Homestead Act of 1862

In 1862, Congress passed the **Homestead Act.** This law gave land to any settler who farmed it for five years. During the 1860s, 1870s, and 1880s, settlers migrated to the West. They settled the Great Plains and much of the Rocky Mountains, the Southwest, and California.

The Development of the Great Plains (1850-1890)

As more people moved west, more farms dotted the land. As more farms were established, more inventions were made to help overcome the difficulties of farming the large tracts of prairie land.

Farm Inventions

1 The steel plow was more efficient than the wooden plow in digging the miles of hard, dry prairie land.

2 Barbed wire kept cattle from wandering into cultivated fields.

3 Windmills provided power to pump water out of wells dug deep underground in prairie lands where rivers and lakes were often hundreds of miles away.

 "When you first came, we were very many, and you were few; now you are many, and we are getting very few, and we are poor." Sioux and Cheyenne leader **Red Cloud** *(1822-1909) spoke these words to describe the Westward Expansion.*

"Once I moved about like the wind. Now I surrender to you and that is all." Apache warrior **Geronimo** *(1829-1909) expressed this view of Native American resettlement.*

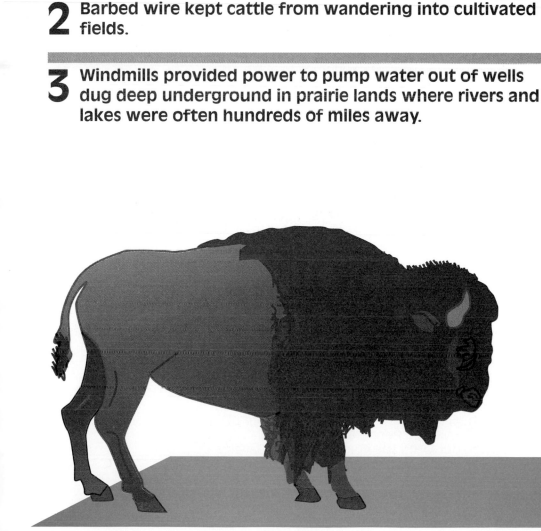

Wheat grew well on the Great Plains and became the main crop. But as prairie land was taken over for crops and grazing land for cattle and sheep, the American Bison was forced from its habitat and nearly driven to extinction.

The Resettlement of Native Americans

In the 1700s and early 1800s, the U.S. government demanded the relocation of Native Americans from the East, South, and Midwest to territories in the West. But as U.S. interests moved further west, so too did Native American relocations. Native Americans resented this, and many fought back. Settlers feared attacks—but not enough to stay off the land.

During the mid-1800s, the U.S. government offered payment or new lands to Native Americans who agreed to move. Sometimes the agreements were honest, but often Native Americans were tricked into agreeing to land deals they didn't understand. Many tribes signed treaties with the U.S. government, wherein they were granted large pieces of land on which no one else could settle. Yet settlers repeatedly broke these treaties and took over the land anyway.

Finally, the U.S. government required that all Native Americans be moved to *reservations*, whether or not they wanted to go. Some went quietly, but others, like the Apaches and the Nez Perce, fought to stay on the lands of their ancestors. Some tribes banded together with tribes of other nations to fight the settlers' spread into ancestral lands, but, in the end, the U.S. Army was too strong for even the greatest war parties assembled by the Native Americans.

In 1890, U.S. troops killed more than 200 Sioux men, women, and children at *Wounded Knee*, South Dakota, even though the Sioux had surrendered peacefully the night before. *Black Elk*, a young Sioux who survived, summed up the feelings of his people. He wrote: "Something else died there . . . A people's dream died there. It was a beautiful dream." By 1900, virtually all Native Americans had been moved to reservations.

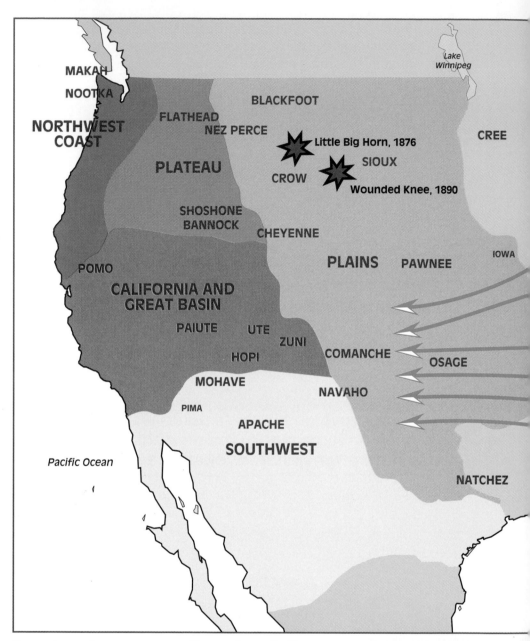

Resentment grew among the various Native American nations as the U.S. government repeatedly broke land treaties. Some Native Americans chose to fight back during what are now called The Indian Wars. The Indian Wars were fought mostly on the Great Plains and in the Southwest. Perhaps the greatest Native American victory was won at Little Big Horn in Montana. Here a combined force of Sioux, Crow, Nez Perce, Blackfoot, and Pawnee defeated the celebrated U.S. Cavalry Brevet General George Armstrong Custer, killing the officer and all 264 soldiers in his 7th Cavalry. Many historians believe the deaths at Custer's Last Stand fueled the slaughter of Native Americans at Wounded Knee.

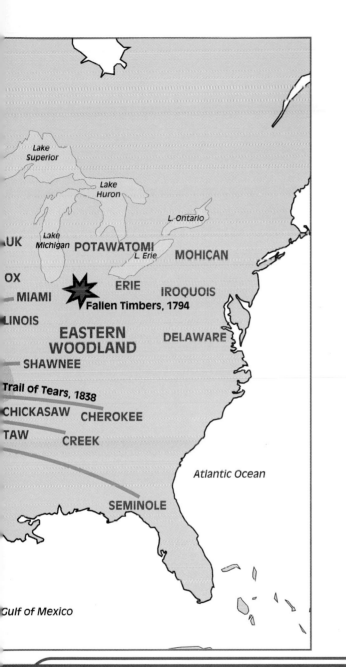

Lake Superior

Lake Huron

L. Ontario

Lake Michigan POTAWATOMI

L. Erie MOHICAN

UK

OX

ERIE

MIAMI IROQUOIS

Fallen Timbers, 1794

LINOIS

EASTERN WOODLAND DELAWARE

SHAWNEE

Trail of Tears, 1838

CHICKASAW CHEROKEE

TAW

CREEK

Atlantic Ocean

SEMINOLE

Gulf of Mexico

The Trail of Tears

The Cherokees lived and farmed for hundreds of years on land in northern Georgia. They wrote their own constitution in 1827, based on the U.S. Constitution, and declared that their territory was an independent nation. However, the state of Georgia would not recognize their independence. It wanted to give the land to whites in a lottery.

President **Andrew Jackson** decided to move the Cherokees to reservations in the West. In 1830, Congress passed the **Indian Removal Act,** which gave the government the right to move the Indians. The Choctaws of Mississippi and the Creeks and Chickasaws of Alabama and Louisiana were moved to Oklahoma during the winters of 1831 and 1832. Many died along the way of cold, disease, and starvation.

John Ross, the Cherokee leader, traveled to Washington to ask the Supreme Court to allow his people to keep their land. The Court ruled in favor of the Cherokees, but the President ignored its decision. He ordered the Cherokees to move. A group of Cherokees signed a treaty agreeing to give up their lands, but other Cherokees said that they did not represent the whole tribe. But in the spring of 1838, Georgia troops forced the Cherokees into camps, which were dirty and did not have enough food and water. About 2,000 Cherokees died.

In the fall of 1838, the move began. It was over 800 miles to Oklahoma, and disease and bitter cold took the lives of another 2,000 Cherokees. By the time they reached their new home, one-fourth of the Cherokee nation had died. That is why the journey became known as the **Trail of Tears**.

More People in Westward Expansion

Catharine Beecher worked throughout the 1840s to improve the lives of women and children. She urged women factory workers to move west to teach pioneer children. She believed that teaching would improve women's status in society. Her sister was **Harriet Beecher Stowe** (see page 55).

Frontiersman **Daniel Boone** became famous for his hunting and sharpshooting skills. In 1775, he and some companions led the way for future settlers to Kentucky. They hacked out the **Wilderness Road** and founded a settlement in Kentucky called Boonesborough.

A Shawnee chief, **Tecumseh,** and his brother, **Tenskwatawa,** tried to unite Native Americans to preserve their culture. Tecumseh led warriors in the bloody uprising at Fallen Timbers in 1794, an early victory in what came to be called the Indian Wars. In 1808, Tecumseh and Tenskwatawa founded a village called Prophetstown in the Indiana Territory.

A Nation Divided (1820-1865)

The Slavery Debate

The 1800s were a time of growth and success for the United States. Yet the North and the South were very different. The South was made up of farms and plantations, where much of the work was done by slaves. The North was an area of small farms and factories, where there were no slaves. As new states entered the Union, the North and South argued over whether they would be **slave states** or **free states.** By the late 1850s, it was clear that the disagreement over slavery would not be resolved peacefully.

The Abolitionist Movement

Around the 1830s, people known as **abolitionists** began to speak out against slavery. The abolitionists wanted to free slaves, and **abolish** (end) slavery. They felt that slavery was wrong—that no person had the right to "own" another human being. They also argued that slavery was against the democratic principles upon which the nation was founded. They pointed out that the Declaration of Independence stated that "all men are created equal" and that all men are entitled to "life, liberty, and the pursuit of happiness." Abolitionists said "all men" included slaves.

Some important abolitionists spread their ideas through newspapers. **Samuel Cornish** published *Freedom's Journal* and **William Lloyd Garrison** published *The Liberator.* Garrison and other abolitionists also formed the **National Antislavery Society** in 1833. Many of its members traveled throughout the country speaking against slavery.

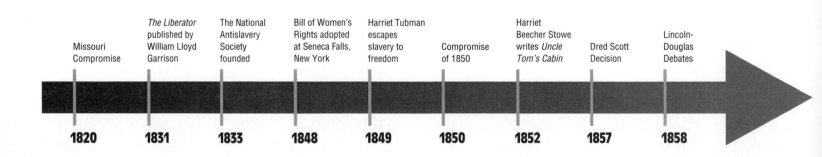

Missouri Compromise	*The Liberator* published by William Lloyd Garrison	The National Antislavery Society founded	Bill of Women's Rights adopted at Seneca Falls, New York	Harriet Tubman escapes slavery to freedom	Compromise of 1850	Harriet Beecher Stowe writes *Uncle Tom's Cabin*	Dred Scott Decision	Lincoln-Douglas Debates
1820	**1831**	**1833**	**1848**	**1849**	**1850**	**1852**	**1857**	**1858**

The Underground Railroad

Abolitionists helped rescue thousands of slaves through the ***Underground Railroad***. This was a system of helping slaves escape from the South into free states or Canada. The "railroad" was really a network of homes and farms where escaped slaves could go for help or shelter. Code words were used for secrecy. A "station" was a hiding place; a "conductor" was the person who guided the slaves to freedom. The Underground Railroad followed a number of routes, but the most heavily traveled one went through Ohio, Indiana, and western Pennsylvania.

Some People in the Abolitionist Movement

Lucretia Mott

Harriet Beecher Stowe

Frederick Douglass

John Brown was a white abolitionist who organized an attack on the Federal arsenal at ***Harpers Ferry***, Virginia, in 1859. He planned to distribute the guns stored there to local slaves and start a revolt across the South. He was captured and hanged.

Lucretia Coffin Mott was a Philadelphia Quaker minister. She helped organize the National Anti-Slavery Society along with ***William Lloyd Garrison.*** Mott became one of the society's most famous speakers. She was also a leader in the struggle for women's right to vote (see p. 92).

An abolitionist who was born a slave in Maryland in 1817, ***Frederick Douglass*** escaped to New York in 1838 and settled in

Massachusetts. He was a talented speaker who founded *The North Star,* one of the first African-American abolitionist newspapers. Douglas wrote in 1870, "the simplest truths often meet the sternest resistance and are slowest in getting general acceptance."

Harriet Beecher Stowe, a teacher and the wife of a minister, wrote the novel *Uncle Tom's Cabin* in 1852. It is about a cruel slave-holder named Simon Legree who whipped Tom, a slave, so badly that he died. The book became a best-seller and convinced many people that slavery should end.

Until she was about thirty years old, ***Sojourner Truth*** was a slave in New York. When all the slaves in New York state were freed in

1827, she traveled the country speaking against slavery. Once, when a man told her that he did not care about her speeches any more than he cared about a flea bite, she replied, "Maybe not, but the Lord willin', I'll keep you scratchin'."

When ***Harriet Tubman*** was twenty-eight years old, she ran away from a Maryland plantation where she was a slave. She became one of the most famous conductors on the ***Underground Railroad***, guiding more than 300 slaves to freedom. Slaveholders offered a reward of forty thousand dollars for her capture. Tubman said, "On my Underground Railroad I never run my train off the track and I have never lost a passenger."

The Missouri Compromise and The Compromise of 1820

The plantations that grew rice, cotton, sugar, and other crops in the South depended on the work of slaves. To make sure that slavery would continue, the South demanded that it be allowed in new western states entering the Union.

When the Missouri Territory applied for admission to the Union in 1819, it applied as a slave state. Missouri's admission would give the South control of the Senate, since there would be twelve slave states to eleven free states. Northern congressmen opposed admitting another slave state. They proposed that Congress abolish slavery in Missouri. This set off a bitter argument between Northerners and Southerners in Congress.

Senator *Henry Clay* of Kentucky was called the Great Compromiser (a *compromise* is a way of settling a disagreement by getting each side to settle for less than it wants). He worked out a solution that kept the number of slave states equal to the number of free states.

The Missouri Compromise

1 **Missouri entered the Union as a slave state.**

2 **Maine entered the Union as a free state.**

3 **Except in Missouri, slavery was banned in all other territories gained in the Louisiana Purchase north of Missouri's southern border.**

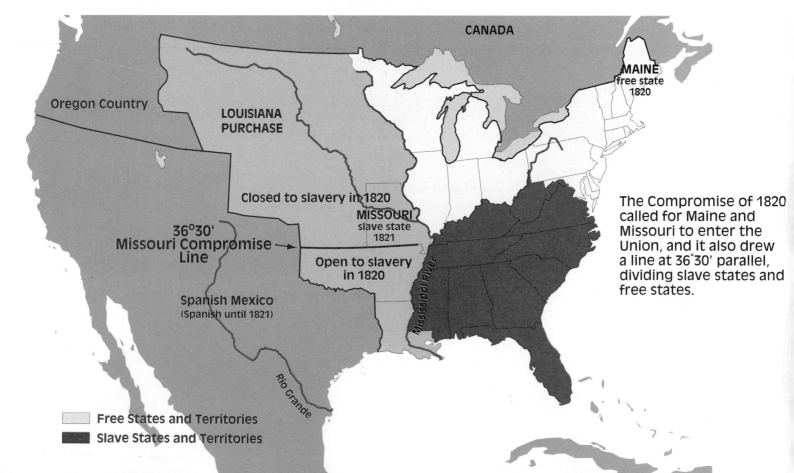

CANADA

MAINE
free state
1820

Oregon Country

LOUISIANA PURCHASE

Closed to slavery in 1820

MISSOURI
slave state
1821

36°30'
Missouri Compromise Line →

Open to slavery in 1820

Mississippi River

Spanish Mexico
(Spanish until 1821)

Rio Grande

Free States and Territories
Slave States and Territories

The Compromise of 1820 called for Maine and Missouri to enter the Union, and it also drew a line at 36°30' parallel, dividing slave states and free states.

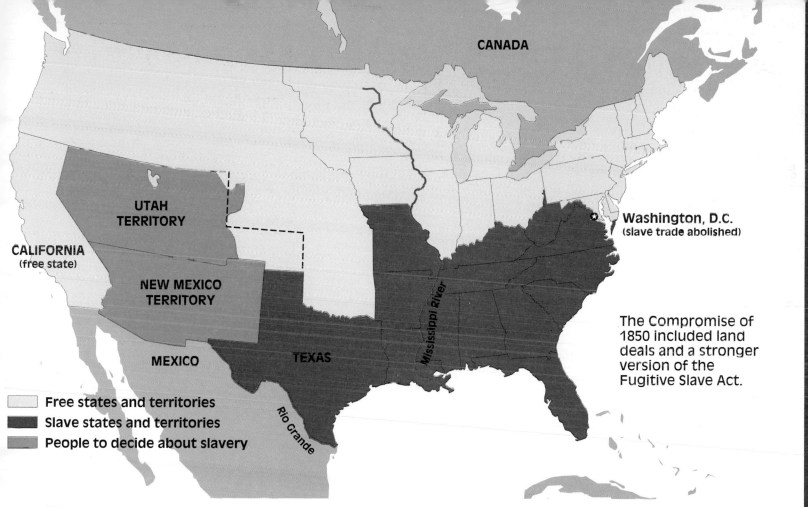

CANADA

UTAH
TERRITORY

CALIFORNIA
(free state)

NEW MEXICO
TERRITORY

MEXICO

TEXAS

Mississippi River

Rio Grande

Washington, D.C.
(slave trade abolished)

The Compromise of
1850 included land
deals and a stronger
version of the
Fugitive Slave Act.

Free states and territories
Slave states and territories
People to decide about slavery

The Compromise of 1850

In 1850, Congress had to decide if California would join the Union as a free or slave state. It also had to decide whether the rest of the territory won in the Mexican War (see p. 48) would be free or not. Once again, **Henry Clay**, the Great Compromiser (see p. 56) along with Senator **Stephen A. Douglas** of Illinois and Senator **Daniel Webster** of Massachusetts, came up with a compromise.

The Compromise of 1850

1 California entered the Union as a free state.

2 The rest of the Mexican territory was divided into New Mexico and Utah. Each state could decide whether to be a slave state or free state. Texas gave up part of its territory to create New Mexico.

3 It was now against the law to buy and sell slaves in Washington, D.C., but not to own slaves.

4 The Fugitive Slave Act made it legal for slave owners to go after and capture runaway slaves who had escaped to the North.

The Dred Scott Decision

In 1857, there was an important national debate over slavery. **Dred Scott** and his wife, **Harriet**, were slaves from Missouri who had moved with their master's family to the free state of Illinois. Later, they all moved back to Missouri, a slave state. Scott went to court to sue for his freedom. Scott claimed that having lived in a free state made him free. The case went before the Supreme Court. Abolitionists (see p. 54) paid Scott's legal fees, and leading abolitionist lawyers argued his case. They wanted to test the legal bounds of slavery, and they were disappointed.

The Supreme Court ruled that Scott could not sue for his freedom because he was property, not a citizen. Chief Justice **Roger Taney** wrote that Scott had "no rights which any white man was bound to respect."

Most Southerners were pleased with the decision. Northern anti-slavery groups were enraged.

The Lincoln-Douglas Debates (1858)

In the 1858 U.S. Senate race, Republican **Abraham Lincoln** of Illinois ran against Democratic Senator **Stephen A. Douglas**, who was up for re-election. Lincoln was unknown. On the night he received the Republican nomination, Lincoln gave a speech in support of the Union. In it he said, "A house divided against itself cannot stand. I believe that this government cannot last as long as America is half slave and half free." He then challenged the pro-slavery Douglas to a series of seven debates. (In a **debate**, two sides argue for or against an issue.) The debates between Lincoln and Douglas drew large crowds and national attention. Although Lincoln lost the Senate race, his performances made him famous throughout the nation. He narrowly defeated Douglas to become President two years later.

Lincoln at the podium during the Lincoln-Douglas debates

THE CIVIL WAR (1861-1865)

Battlelines

A *civil war* is a war between different groups of people of the same nation. The American Civil War was fought between the North and the South. It was triggered by the election of Republican President **Abraham Lincoln** in 1860. Lincoln wanted to keep the Union together and to end the spread of slavery to new states.

Secession

After Lincoln was elected, southern states began to **secede** from, or leave, the Union. Eleven slave states formed their own government, called the **Confederacy.** They elected **Jefferson Davis** as their president.

Border States

Some slave states—**Missouri**, **Kentucky**, and **Maryland**—did not secede, although they continued to have slaves. The western part of Virginia opposed slavery. When Virginia seceded, the state was reorganized, and the western portion became **West Virginia**. These four states are often called **border states**.

Abraham Lincoln

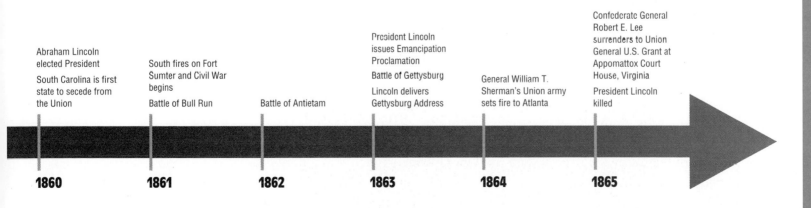

1860	1861	1862	1863	1864	1865
Abraham Lincoln elected President — South Carolina is first state to secede from the Union	South fires on Fort Sumter and Civil War begins — Battle of Bull Run	Battle of Antietam	President Lincoln issues Emancipation Proclamation — Battle of Gettysburg — Lincoln delivers Gettysburg Address	General William T. Sherman's Union army sets fire to Atlanta	Confederate General Robert E. Lee surrenders to Union General U.S. Grant at Appomattox Court House, Virginia — President Lincoln killed

The End of Slavery

More than 600,000 Americans died in the Civil War, more than in any other U.S. war before or since. The Confederate defeat led to the end of slavery throughout the United States and restored the Union, although much of the South was destroyed.

Causes of the Civil War

1 **Slavery.** Although most Southerners did not own slaves, and most Northerners were not abolitionists, slavery was at the heart of most major issues dividing the North and the South.

2 **Ways of life.** In both the North and the South, most people lived on small farms. But in the North, there were several large cities where many people worked in factories. In the South there were many plantations worked by slaves.

3 **Free labor vs. slave labor.** The Northern economy was based on free laborers who could work where they chose and received a wage. The Southern economy was based on slave laborers who were not free to leave and received food and lodging but no wages.

4 **States' rights.** The North thought that no state had a right to leave the Union, or secede. The South argued that a state could leave the Union if it voted to do so.

The Confederate Government

President	Jefferson Davis (Mississippi)
Vice President	Alexander Hamilton Stephens (Georgia)
Secretary of State	Robert Toombs (Georgia)
Secretary of War	Leroy Pope Walker (Alabama)
Secretary of Treasury	Christopher Memminger (South Carolina)
Attorney General	Judah P. Benjamin (Louisiana)
Secretary of Navy	Stephen Mallory (Florida)
Postmaster General	John H. Reagan (Texas)
Capital	Montgomery, Alabama; then Richmond, Virginia

Map labels:

Washington Territory
OREGON
Nevada Territory
CALIFORNIA
Utah Territory
Dakota Territory
Nebraska Territory
Colorado Territory
KANSAS
New Mexico Territory
Unorganized Territory
MINNESOTA
WISCONSIN
MICHIGAN
IOWA
ILLINOIS
MISSOURI
ARKANSAS
TEXAS
LOUISIANA
INDIANA
OHIO
KENTUCKY
TENNESSEE
MISSISSIPPI
ALABAMA
GEORGIA
FLORIDA
NEW HAMPSHIRE
VERMONT
MAINE
MASSACHUSETTS
NEW YORK
RHODE ISLAND
PENNSYLVANIA
CONNECTICUT
NEW JERSEY
DELAWARE
MARYLAND
WEST VIRGINIA
VIRGINIA
NORTH CAROLINA
SOUTH CAROLINA

Legend:

- Union Free States
- Union Territories
- Slave States Remaining in the Union
- Confederate States
- Confederate Territories

THE CIVIL WAR (1861-1865)

THE CONFEDERACY

State	Date Seceded	Date Readmitted
1. South Carolina	Dec. 20, 1860	June 25, 1868
2. Mississippi	Jan. 9, 1861	Feb. 23, 1870
3. Florida	Jan. 10, 1861	June 25, 1868
4. Alabama	Jan. 11, 1861	June 25, 1868
5. Georgia	Jan. 19, 1861	July 15, 1870
6. Louisiana	Jan. 26, 1861	June 25, 1868
7. Texas	Feb. 1, 1861	March 30, 1870
8. Arkansas	May 6, 1861	June 22, 1868
9. North Carolina	May 20, 1861	June 25, 1868
10. Virginia	Apr. 17, 1861	Jan. 26, 1870
11. Tennessee	June 8, 1861	July 24, 1866

Chronology of the Civil War

1861

March 4	Abraham Lincoln inaugurated as President
April 12	Civil War begins when Confederates attack Fort Sumter, South Carolina
July 21	First Battle of Bull Run, Virginia, also called First Manassas

1862

September 16-17	Battle of Antietam (Sharpsburg), Maryland
September 23	President Lincoln issues preliminary Emancipation Proclamation freeing slaves in South as of January 1, 1863
December 13	Battle of Fredericksburg, Virginia

1862

February 16	Battle at Fort Donelson, Tennessee
March 9	Naval battle between Union Monitor and Confederate Merrimac in the Atlantic Ocean. Merrimac withdraws
April 6-7	Battle of Shiloh, Tennessee
April 25	Union Admiral David G. Farragut captures New Orleans, Louisiana
May 31-June 1	Battle of Fair Oaks (Seven Pines), Virginia
June 25-July 1	Seven Days' Battles, Maryland and Virginia

1863

January 1	President Lincoln issues Emancipation Proclamation
May 2-4	Battle of Chancellorsville, Virginia
July 1-3	Battle of Gettysburg, Pennsylvania; Union victory marks turning point in the war
July 4	Union forces win siege of Vicksburg, Mississippi
September 19-20	Battle of Chickamauga, Georgia
November 19	President Lincoln delivers Gettysburg Address to dedicate battlefield
November 23-25	Battle of Chattanooga, Tennessee

1864

March 9	Gen. Grant becomes General-in-Chief of Union armies
May 5-6	Battle of the Wilderness, Virginia
May 8-12	Battle of Spotsylvania, Virginia, Court House
June 15-18	Battle of Petersburg, Virginia
July 11-12	Confederate raid under Gen. Jubal Early almost reaches Washington
July 30	Battle of the Crater, Petersburg, Virginia
August 5	Naval battle of Mobile Bay, Alabama
September 2	Gen. William T. Sherman occupies Atlanta, Georgia
November 8	Abraham Lincoln re-elected President
November 15	Sherman begins his March to the Sea
December 15-16	Battle of Nashville, Tennessee
December 21	Sherman occupies Savannah, Georgia

1865

February 6	Gen. Robert E. Lee becomes General-in-Chief of Confederate armies
March 25	Confederate attempt to break out of Petersburg, Virginia, fails
April 2	Confederates retreat from Richmond, Virginia
April 9	Gen. Lee surrenders to Gen. Grant at Appomattox Court House
April 14	President Lincoln assassinated
April 26	Presidential assassin John Wilkes Booth shot and killed
May 4	Last Confederate army surrenders

THE CIVIL WAR (1861-1865)

Advantages of the North

1 About 10 million more people — 22 million compared with 9 million free and 3.5 million slaves in the South

2 More factories to produce guns, uniforms, military supplies

3 Navy and merchant marine

4 Rail system twice as large as the South's to move troops and supplies

5 Most of the banks and cash in the United States

Advantages of the South

1 Better military leaders

2 Most of the war fought in the South on familiar terrain

3 More skilled horsemen and riflemen

Total deaths: 620,000
Union deaths: 360,000
Confederate deaths: 260,000

Clara Barton

Known as the "Angel of the Battlefields," **Clara Barton** organized the nursing of wounded Union troops throughout the Civil War. In 1881, she founded the American Red Cross.

Ulysses S. Grant was the sixth general to head the Union forces. He was a graduate of the U.S. Military Academy at West Point but not a model soldier. Grant nevertheless was a brilliant military leader and a stubborn fighter. He was later elected President for two terms.

The general of the Confederate forces, ***Robert E. Lee,*** was a graduate of West Point Military Academy and a hero of the Mexican War (see p. 48). Lincoln offered him command of the Union forces, but Lee refused. Although Lee disapproved of both slavery and secession, he could not bring himself to fight against his fellow Southerners.

Ulysses S. Grant

Mary S. Peake was a free African American who set up a school in Hampton, Virginia, in 1861. Her school was for former slaves who fell behind Union lines as the army advanced.

More People in the Civil War

Robert Shaw was a Union officer from a wealthy abolitionist family in Massachusetts. He was commander of the Massachusetts 54th Regiment, one of the first African-American units to serve in the Civil War. In 1863, he was killed in the Battle of Fort Wagner.

Robert Smalls was an African-American seaman who was forced to serve on the *Planter*, a Confederate gunboat. He and the crew took over the boat and escaped the Confederates, then sailed the boat to the Union blockade, where he surrendered it. His daring feat was widely publicized, and Congress voted to give him a large reward.

At the outbreak of the war, ***Sally Tompkins*** opened a hospital in Richmond, Virginia, which earned an outstanding record for saving the lives of wounded Confederate soldiers. Confederate President ***Jefferson Davis*** presented her with the commission of captain in the army.

Robert E. Lee

RECONSTRUCTION AND THE BIRTH OF CIVIL RIGHTS (1865-1877)

1 Reconstruction

The twelve-year period after the Civil War is known as *Reconstruction*. During this period, the nation faced the problems of rebuilding the South and reuniting the states. Presidents *Abraham Lincoln* and *Andrew Johnson* wanted to be gentle on former Confederates. However, many of the southern states began passing laws that took freedom from African Americans. Congress wanted the South to accept the end of slavery. Led by a group known as the *Radical Republicans*, Congress wanted to make sure that freed slaves were safe and that they could make a living and be full citizens.

Historians divide Reconstruction into two stages. The first, from 1865 to 1866, was controlled by the Presidents. The second, from 1866 to 1877, was controlled by Congress and is called *Radical Reconstruction*.

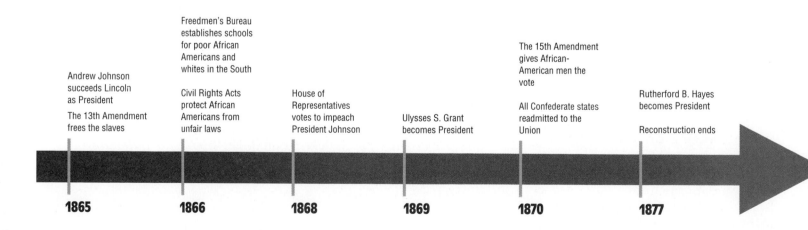

Andrew Johnson succeeds Lincoln as President

The 13th Amendment frees the slaves

Freedmen's Bureau establishes schools for poor African Americans and whites in the South

Civil Rights Acts protect African Americans from unfair laws

House of Representatives votes to impeach President Johnson

Ulysses S. Grant becomes President

The 15th Amendment gives African-American men the vote

All Confederate states readmitted to the Union

Rutherford B. Hayes becomes President

Reconstruction ends

1865   1866   1868   1869   1870   1877

The Presidential Plan

In March 1865, President **Abraham Lincoln** signed a law passed by Congress that created the **Freedmen's Bureau**. Its purpose was to feed both blacks and whites in the South, to help former slaves find jobs, and to protect them from discrimination.

After Lincoln was assassinated, his vice president, **Andrew Johnson**, a Democrat from Tennessee, became President. He disagreed with Republicans in Congress about how to bring the Confederate states back into the Union and how to treat their leaders. Johnson pardoned most southerners including Confederate officials and army officers. These pardons permitted former Confederates to vote and hold office. Johnson even pardoned **Alexander Stephens**, the Confederate vice president, so that he could serve in Congress.

In 1865, four former Confederate generals, six Confederate cabinet members, and fifty-eight Confederate congressmen, as well as Stephens, had been elected U.S. Representatives. Radical Republicans did not like this. Congress set up a committee to decide if these members should be seated.

Black Codes

Although slavery was abolished in 1865, African Americans were not given full rights as citizens. Southern states passed laws to keep former slaves from: voting, testifying against whites in court, serving on juries, and joining the militia (state army forces). These laws were known as **black codes**.

Radical Reconstruction

In order to re-enter the Union, Congress required each Southern state to ratify the 14th Amendment. Only Tennessee did. Congress divided the South—except Tennessee—into five military districts. An army general and federal troops were sent to each district. Southern states were required to hold conventions with both black and white delegates to rewrite their state constitutions.

Carpetbaggers and Scalawags

After the war, many Northerners moved to the South. Some were missionaries and teachers who went to help the former slaves and suffering farmers. Others went to take advantage of the disorder. These people were called **carpetbaggers** because many carried suitcases made of carpet material.

Southern Democrats used the word **scalawag**, meaning rascal, to refer to Southern whites who supported the Radical Republicans during Reconstruction.

Reconstruction Amendments and Laws

Led by Representative *Thaddeus Stevens* of Pennsylvania and Senator *Charles Sumner* of Massachusetts, Congress passed three amendments to the Constitution and several laws about the treatment of former slaves.

Reconstruction Legislation

1 The 13th Amendment freed the slaves (passed February 1865; ratified in December 1865).

2 The Freedmen's Bureau (1866) was established by law.

3 The Civil Rights Act of 1866 declared that all persons born in the United States were citizens.

4 The 14th Amendment made all former slaves U.S. citizens (passed June 1866; ratified July 1868).

5 The 15th Amendment gave African-American men the right to vote (passed February 1869; ratified March 1870).

6 Force Acts of 1870 and 1871 (Ku Klux Klan Acts) protected African Americans from acts of terrorism.

7 The Civil Rights Act of 1875 was aimed at ending Jim Crow laws (see p. 69). It was overturned by the Supreme Court in 1883.

8 The Compromise of 1877 settled an undecided Presidential election and ended Reconstruction. In return for making Republican Rutherford B. Hayes President, Southern Democrats were promised that federal troops would be removed from the South. Democrat Samuel Tilden lost the election. He had enough popular votes to win but not enough electoral votes (see p. 119).

African American Officeholders

Between 1869 and 1876, fourteen black men were elected to the House of Representatives. Two others, **Hiram R. Revels** and **Blanche K. Bruce**, were elected to the Senate. Some of these men had been born slaves. Others had been born free, and several had attended college. During Reconstruction, more than 600 African Americans served in state legislatures.

The Ku Klux Klan

The Ku Klux Klan was formed in Pulaski, Tennessee, in 1866 by a group of Confederate veterans who claimed to be the ghosts of Confederate soldiers. The Klan was a secret society, which appeared in public dressed in white robes and hoods that covered members' faces. The Klan believed in the supremacy of the white race and tried to terrorize African Americans and carpetbaggers and scalawags who supported them. To keep African Americans from voting, the Klan burned their homes and lynched (hanged) them. By 1867, there were local units of the Klan in every state from Virginia to Texas.

Jim Crow Laws

Jim Crow laws were passed by southern states to legalize segregation. They created separate areas for blacks and whites in public waiting rooms, restaurants, schools, and hospitals. The name *Jim Crow* comes from a popular minstrel song, *Jump, Jim Crow*. **Minstrels** were usually white people who put black paint on their faces. They sang and danced and acted happy-go-lucky. There were Jim Crow laws until the 1960s in many places of the United States.

Samuel Clemens, better known by his penname Mark Twain, was a harsh but humorous critic of U.S. society and government. His masterpiece, *The Adventures of Huckleberry Finn* (1884), attacks the slave system that for years was a way of life in the South. Clemens also criticized Jim Crow laws and the acts of the state and federal governments that he found "undemocratic."

The Impeachment of Andrew Johnson

Congress and President *Andrew Johnson* fought bitterly over Reconstruction. Congress passed laws and the President *vetoed* (said no to) them. Most of the laws were passed over his vetoes.

In 1867, Congress passed the *Tenure of Office Act*. It prevented President Johnson from removing government officials without the consent of Congress. Johnson said the Constitution did not give Congress the right to pass such a law. To test the law, Johnson removed Secretary of War *Edwin M. Stanton* from office. Next, the House of Representatives charged the President with "high crimes and misdemeanors" and voted to impeach him. *Impeachment* is an indictment, or charge, of a high government official for a crime (see p. 119).

The Senate held a trial and heard the evidence in spring 1868, but Johnson's opponents did not have the two-thirds majority needed to convict him. Johnson served out his term as President.

2 The Birth of the Civil Rights Movement

After Reconstruction (see pp. 66-70), African Americans were still badly treated. Blacks and whites were **segregated** (kept separate) in public places. Former slaves often worked as **sharecroppers**. They lived on and farmed land owned by someone else and were given back a share of the crops in return. Elsewhere, African Americans got the lowest paying jobs and had little opportunity to move up.

Black leaders did not always agree on how to deal with this inequality. The very popular African-American leader **Booker T. Washington** believed that learning how to make a living was the first step toward equality. He founded **Tuskegee Institute**, an industrial school for African Americans in Alabama.

W.E.B. DuBois, the first African American to receive a doctoral degree from Harvard University, said that without equal rights, making a living was meaningless. He helped found the **National Association for the Advancement of Colored People** (NAACP) in 1909. Its members included both blacks and whites. The NAACP became a major force for civil rights for African Americans throughout the twentieth century.

More People in Reconstruction

Blanche K. Bruce was the first African-American senator to serve a full term in the Senate (from 1875 to 1881). He represented Mississippi. Bruce was born a slave in Virginia, escaped to the North, and attended Oberlin College in Ohio. When his political career was over, he became a planter in Mississippi.

Thaddeus Stevens was a white abolitionist Representative from Pennsylvania. He studied law at Dartmouth College. After the Civil War ended, he pushed for more rights for African Americans. Under his leadership, Congress passed the 14th Amendment (see pp. 120-121).

Born in 1869, **Ida B. Wells** was an African American from the South who led a movement to educate the American public about lynchings and to make sure people were punished for them. She edited and published a newspaper, *The Memphis Free Speech*, as well as many pamphlets.

INDUSTRIALIZATION (1850-1900)

1 Industrial Revolution

Before the Civil War

In the early 1800s, manufacturing products changed from handmade to machine-made. This period is called the *First Industrial Revolution*. It changed small businesses into huge manufacturing companies.

Almost all U.S. industry was in the North before the Civil War. Many Northerners worked in factories. These factories had large machines that produced clothes, guns, or farm tools much faster than individual workers could. Southerners continued to farm for a living. The ability to make products quickly by machine was a major advantage for the North in the Civil War.

After the Civil War

A much more powerful *Second Industrial Revolution* took place after the Civil War. The economy of the entire nation began to move away from farming toward industry. Companies began to get much larger and production was greatly increased. Because of industry, the nation's wealth grew by five-and-one-half times between 1860 and 1900. Americans moved from rural areas to cities to take jobs in factories. Immigrants (see pp. 78-79) coming into the United States from all over the world also found factory jobs.

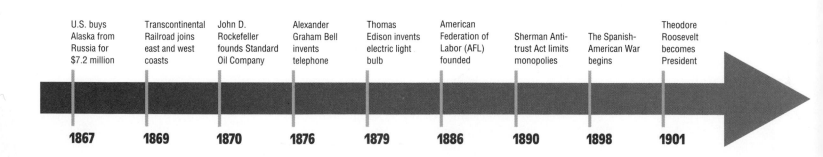

U.S. buys Alaska from Russia for $7.2 million	Transcontinental Railroad joins east and west coasts	John D. Rockefeller founds Standard Oil Company	Alexander Graham Bell invents telephone	Thomas Edison invents electric light bulb	American Federation of Labor (AFL) founded	Sherman Anti-trust Act limits monopolies	The Spanish-American War begins	Theodore Roosevelt becomes President
1867	**1869**	**1870**	**1876**	**1879**	**1886**	**1890**	**1898**	**1901**

Effects of the Industrial Revolution

Positive Effects

- More jobs and opportunities were created.

- Inventions, like the railroad and the electric light bulb, made life more comfortable.

Negative Effects

- Only a few people got wealthy—often at the expense of workers.

- Living and working conditions in the industrial cities were often poor and unhealthy.

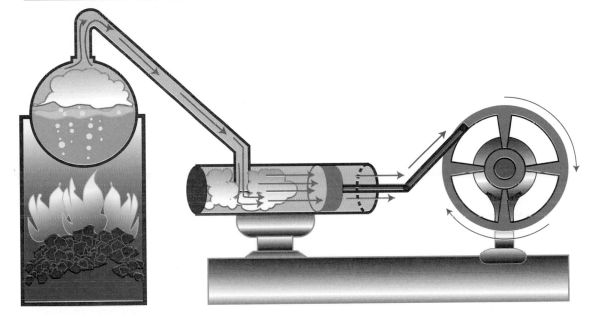

Scottish inventor James Watt worked as a mathematical instrument maker at the University of Glasgow when he became interested in improving the steam engine. By 1769, he patented his new steam engine designs and, by the mid-1780s, put his idea into production.

In Watt's *reciprocating steam engine*, steam pushed a piston to and fro. The engine worked very efficiently and could be used to run large machines created for a variety of different jobs. These large machines replaced the work of humans to usher in the Industrial Revolution.

2 Robber Barons and Monopolies

During the rise of industry, business owners tried to create *monopolies* by buying up all the companies that competed with their own. By doing this, a company would increase its profits. Customers had to pay the higher prices because the products weren't available from any other manufacturers.

Robber barons were big businessmen of the late 1800s. They became very wealthy by driving small companies out of business. They charged high prices, took advantage of workers, and bribed government officials. On the other hand, they provided better services, improved the quality of their products, and built up the nation's industries.

Often the government helped big business get around the law. Some government officials agreed to help the robber barons because they thought that industrialization was good for the country. Others were dishonest and took bribes to pass laws that were favorable to big business. In both cases, the government sided with the interests of big business instead of with the average worker.

BIG BUSINESSMEN OF THE LATE 1800s AND THEIR INDUSTRIES

Cornelius Vanderbilt	Railroads
John D. Rockefeller	Oil
Andrew Carnegie	Steel
Gustavus Swift	Meat packing
Philip D. Armour	Meat packing
Charles A. Pillsbury	Flour milling
James B. Duke	Cigarette manufacturing
Andrew W. Mellon	Aluminum

 When a business gets rid of all its competitors, it has a monopoly. *When companies are joined to limit competition in an industry, they form a* trust.

3 The Rise of Labor

A *union* is a group of workers who join together to bargain with the owners of companies. *Management* represents the owners' interest. The purpose of a union is to give workers greater influence over management. Because groups of workers acting together have more power to win their demands than one individual, printers, stonecutters, machinists, and others had formed craft unions by the 1850s.

The rise of unions came after the *Civil War* (see pp. 59-65). Industries were expanding, and needed more workers. There were seventy-nine unions in twenty states in 1863. By 1864, there were 170. The first important national labor federation, or group of unions, was formed in 1866. It was headed by *William H. Sylvis*. The federation favored reforms, such as the eight-hour workday and an end to child labor.

EARLY LABOR UNIONS

Knights of Labor Male workers who cut clothing in Philadelphia, Pennsylvania formed a union in 1869. Their leader was *Uriah S. Stephens*. He called his organization the Noble Order of the Knights of Labor. Originally a secret organization, it became a national federation in 1879. It was the first to form local units, or assemblies, in different areas for all workers. It had more than 700,000 members in 1886.

American Federation of Labor (AFL) This national labor federation was formed in 1886 in Columbus, Ohio. Its first president was *Samuel Gompers*, leader of the Cigar Makers' Union. The AFL gave the unions the right to organize workers around a specific job or craft. It developed collective bargaining practices and was strengthened when the *National Labor Relations Act* passed in 1935 (see p. 76).

Industrial Workers of the World (IWW) The IWW was founded by *Eugene V. Debs, William D. (Big Bill) Haywood, Daniel DeLeon*, and others in 1905. Its members were nicknamed the *Wobblies*. The main purpose of the Wobblies was to overthrow *capitalism* (the system where individuals, not the government, own most businesses and factories, and workers earn a wage). They favored strikes and other actions over collective bargaining. Other unions opposed the Wobblies, and they eventually broke up.

Congress of Industrial Organizations (CIO) The CIO was founded in Washington, D.C., in 1935 by *John L. Lewis*, head of the United Mine

John L. Lewis

Workers. Its purpose was to represent all workers of one industry in a single trade union. Before the CIO, one industry, such as steel, might have twenty or more craft unions represented in a single factory. The AFL and the CIO merged in 1955. *George Meany* was named the first president of the combined organizations.

UNION TERMS

Arbitration An agreement by labor and management to allow a third person to settle disputes.

Union shop A workplace where workers must join a union after being hired.

Collective bargaining Where union representatives negotiate with management in the interests of union workers.

Grievance A complaint about wages, schedules, or other matters by labor against management.

Lockout An employer's refusal to let employees into the workplace unless they accept management's terms.

Mediate To step in to settle a dispute.

Negotiate To discuss how much of something, such as work, will be exchanged for something else, such as wages or benefits.

Pickets Union workers who stand outside a workplace to discourage the public from doing business with the company and other workers from working there.

Strike or walkout A refusal to work in order to get certain benefits or agreements from management.

Strikebreaker A person hired by an employer to do the work of an employee who is on strike.

4 Labor Legislation

Many laws were passed in the nineteenth and twentieth centuries to deal with relations between labor and management.

Labor Legislation

- **Erdman Act (1898): Provided arbitration and mediation to settle disputes between unions and employers.**

- **Adamson Act (1916): Established an eight-hour day for workers on interstate railroads.**

- **National Labor Relations Act (Wagner Act) (1935): Guaranteed workers the right to organize and bargain collectively.**

- **Labor-Management Relations Act (Taft-Hartley Act of 1947): Restricted strikes that endangered the nation's safety, health, or welfare.**

THEODORE ROOSEVELT and Trust Busting

Theodore Roosevelt became the 26th President after *William McKinley* was assassinated in 1901. Roosevelt said that he wanted to give everyone — seller and consumer — a "square deal." Roosevelt and politicians like him were called *Progressives*. They wanted to give working people some protection against big business. Progressives thought that breaking up the trusts would result in more competition and better prices for average Americans.

In 1902, Roosevelt decided to make an example of one of the trusts. Under a law called the *Sherman Anti-Trust Act*, he sued a railroad trust called the Northern Securities Company. Two years later, the Supreme Court ruled against the trust. Roosevelt's tough stand against big business made him very popular.

In 1901, Roosevelt coined the expression: "Speak softly and carry a big stick." Against big business, Roosevelt was a man of his words.

Theodore Roosevelt

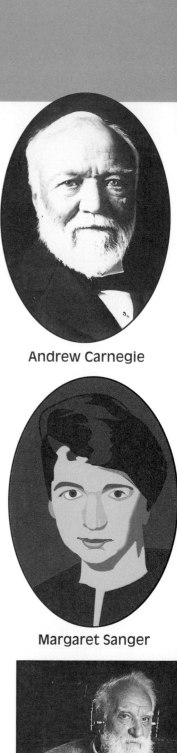

Andrew Carnegie

Margaret Sanger

More People from the Age of Industry

Jane Addams was a social worker who worked to improve conditions for Chicago's poor immigrants. She founded *Hull House,* a settlement house where immigrants could take English, music, and job training classes.

The first telephone was invented in 1876 by *Alexander Graham Bell.* His invention grew out of experiments he was conducting on ways to teach deaf people to speak. Bell also believed in the power of pictures to teach. He founded the *National Geographic* magazine.

The son of poor Scottish immigrants, *Andrew Carnegie* became the richest man in the world by 1901 by investing in the steel industry and selling rails to railroads. After he had made his fortune, Carnegie started giving it away. He paid for 2,811 public libraries in the United States. He also built Carnegie Hall in New York City and founded Carnegie-Mellon University in Pittsburgh, Pennsylvania.

Alexander
Graham
Bell

Eugene V. Debs was the leader of America's first industrial union, the IWW (see p. 75). In 1894, he became a hero to working people when he went to jail for six months rather than call off the Pullman Railroad Strike, the first major railroad strike in the United States. Debs was a socialist (one who believes in government, rather than private, ownership of factories and other parts of the economic system) who ran unsuccessfully for President five times.

Although as a boy he was taken out of school for making trouble, *Thomas Alva Edison* got rich from his many inventions. Among them were the light bulb, the phonograph, an early movie camera, and an improved typewriter. According to Edison, "genius is 1% inspiration and 99% perspiration."

Henry Ford left his family's farm to become a mechanic in Detroit when he was sixteen years old. In his spare time, he worked on an idea for a horseless carriage. By 1893, he had built a working two-cylinder engine. By 1896, he had created a 500-pound car that ran. Ford's real achievement was the Model T. With it, he realized his dream of building a car so inexpensive that average people could own one.

In 1883, African American *Jan Matzeliger* invented the lasting machine, which revolutionized the manufacture of shoes. The lasting machine was adopted in factories around the world.

Elijah McCoy was an African American who worked on machines that lubricated (greased) engines. He patented a cup that became used on railroads and steam ships that made it unnecessary to stop machines in order to grease them.

John D. Rockefeller ran one of the most famous trusts (see p. 74) in American history, the Standard Oil Company. In 1870, Rockefeller formed the Standard Oil Company of Ohio. By 1879, he had managed either to buy most of his competitors' companies or to drive them out of business. By controlling the major oil companies, Rockefeller could set the price of oil. Rockefeller's trust controlled over ninety percent of the country's oil refineries. Rockefeller became one of the richest men in the world.

Margaret Sanger was a feminist (see pp. 92-93). While working as a nurse in a poor immigrant neighborhood in New York City, Sanger became convinced that having too many babies kept families poor. She devoted her life to making information about birth control available to women.

5 Immigration

About twenty-eight million immigrants came to the United States between 1830 and 1910. Most U.S. immigrants came from North, Central, and Southern Europe. From 1870 to 1890, approximately 8.5 million new immigrants came to the United States. The greatest number—12.5 million immigrants—came between 1891 to 1910.

Immigration Waves

Some immigrants came to the United States to find religious freedom. Others came in the hope of making a better life for themselves and their families. Others came to escape governments that offered little freedom. A few came just for adventure. Between the 17th and 19th centuries, many people came to this country because they had been sold into slavery.

In 1790, the U.S. government took a *census*, or count, of all people in the country. Except for the Native Americans, all the people came from Europe or Africa.

An immigrant is someone who comes into a new country or region to live. An emigrant is someone who leaves.

To become citizens, immigrants had to live in the United States for at least five years.

1790 Census
- **Total population of the United States: 3,929,000**

- **Two of every three people came from Britain**

- **One of every five people came from Africa**

- **The rest of the people came mainly from Scotland, Ireland, Germany, Holland, and France**

From 1820 to 1930, more than thirty-seven million people came to the United States. This was the largest movement of people in the history of the world. All of these immigrants help make America what it is today.

Immigrants arriving at Ellis Island in New York Harbor

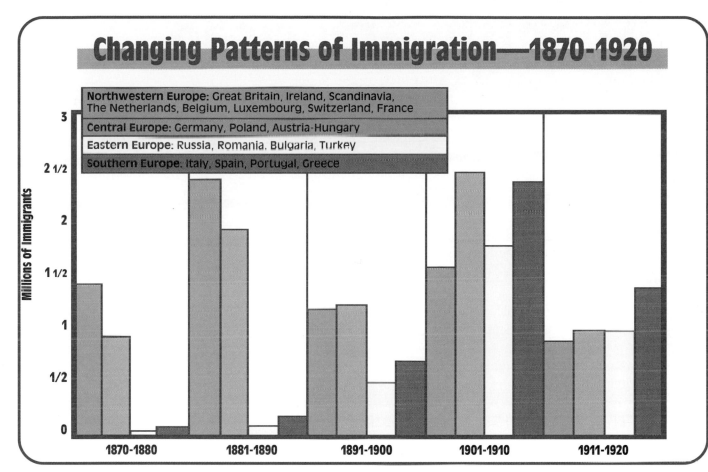

Changing Patterns of Immigration—1870-1920

Northwestern Europe: Great Britain, Ireland, Scandinavia, The Netherlands, Belgium, Luxembourg, Switzerland, France
Central Europe: Germany, Poland, Austria-Hungary
Eastern Europe: Russia, Romania, Bulgaria, Turkey
Southern Europe: Italy, Spain, Portugal, Greece

Immigrants who arrived in the United States from 1870 on populated cities and created a new labor force for industry.

Growth of Cities

Before 1870, less than one in four people lived in cities. The others lived on farms or in small towns and villages. This began to change with industrialization. In the early and mid-1900s, more and more African Americans migrated to northern cities. New waves of immigrants from Europe and Asia also settled in the port cities of the East and West coasts.

AMERICANS LIVING IN CITIES AND ON FARMS

DATE	CITIES	FARMS
1880	28%	72%
1910	45%	55%
1940	56%	44%
1970	75%	25%

INDUSTRIALIZATION (1850-1900)

6 The Spanish-American War of 1898

In January 1898, the Caribbean island of Cuba was fighting against Spain to gain independence. The U.S. battleship *Maine* made a "friendly visit" to Cuba to protect Americans and their property on the island. Many Spanish thought it showed that the United States supported the rebel Cubans.

On the night of February 15, a huge explosion destroyed the ship. It sank in minutes and killed 260 crew members. The cause of the blast is still unknown, but many angry Americans blamed the Spanish.

Two New York City papers—the *New York Journal,* owned by **William Randolph Hearst**, and the *New York World*, owned by **Joseph Pulitzer**— were competing for readers and profits. They used the explosion of the *Maine* as a tool in their battle. They exaggerated what happened in order to get New Yorkers to buy more papers. Newspaper headlines of "Remember the *Maine*!" and articles called for the United States to declare war against Spain. Today we call this exaggerated storytelling **yellow journalism**.

President **William McKinley** did not want to rush into war, but the press and public opinion were against him. Finally, he declared war against Spain in April 1898. The Spanish-American War started in the Philippine Islands in the Pacific Ocean — halfway around the world. The Philippines were also a Spanish colony. After a brief battle, the Spanish surrendered the islands to the U.S. Navy on May 1, 1898. Back in Cuba, U.S. Cavalry troops, called **Rough Riders,** under the leadership of **Theodore Roosevelt**, won the Battle of San Juan Hill. The United States destroyed the Spanish fleet two days later.

Rough Riders in action at the Battle of San Juan Hill

Causes of the Spanish-American War

1 The U.S. battleship <u>Maine</u> in Cuba's Havana harbor was sunk mysteriously on February 15, 1898.

2 Many Americans thought the United States should help the Cuban rebels gain independence from Spain.

3 Other Americans wanted Spain out of Cuba so that the United States could control the island and protect U.S. business interests there.

4 American newspapers stirred people up by printing sensational stories.

Theodore Roosevelt in his Rough Rider uniform

Results of the Spanish-American War

1 Cuba got limited independence from Spain.

2 The United States gained an empire of Spain's old possessions—Puerto Rico, Guam, and the Philippines.

3 The United States paid Spain $20 million for the Philippines.

4 Theodore Roosevelt became a national hero. President McKinley chose him to be his running mate in the next election.

5 The U.S. victory demonstrated the growing importance of the United States as a leader in international affairs.

7 New Territories Acquired by the United States

Alaska

Alaska was bought from Russia in 1867 for 7.2 million dollars by Secretary of State *William Seward*. Alaska was often called "Seward's Folly" because many people thought it was a barren icebox. Alaska became a state in 1959.

Hawaii

Hawaii was *annexed* (joined to the United States) in 1898. *Queen Liliuokalani* was overthrown in 1893 by revolutionaries, who were mostly Americans. When they asked to be annexed by the United States, President *Grover Cleveland* delayed because he thought most native Hawaiians wanted independence. After the election of 1896, President William McKinley made Hawaii a U.S. territory. It became a state in 1959.

Panama Canal Zone

The United States built a canal across the Isthmus of Panama that connected the Atlantic and the Pacific Oceans. (An *isthmus* is a narrow strip of land between two bodies of water.) The Panama Canal reduced the trip around South America by 8,000 miles when it opened in 1914. The labor was made possible by the work of Dr. *William Gorgas*. He was able to clear out the breeding places of mosquitoes that carried yellow fever. The disease had killed so many workers that it threatened the project. *George W. Goethals*, an army engineer, finished the canal, which was one of the greatest engineering feats of all time. The United States agreed to pay Panama ten million dollars and an annual rent of 250,000 dollars to control the Canal Zone. In 1978, the United States signed two treaties, turning over the Panama Canal to the Republic of Panama by the year 2000.

Puerto Rico

Puerto Rico became a U.S. territory in 1900 after the Spanish-American War (see pp. 80-81). In 1952, Puerto Rico was made a commonwealth, which meant that it could elect its own governor and pass and enforce its own laws. Puerto Ricans are U.S. citizens, but they cannot vote in Presidential elections or elect Members of Congress. They are subject to U.S. laws but do not have to pay income tax. In 1993, Puerto Rico voted to remain a commonwealth rather than become a state of the United States or an independent country.

Theodore Roosevelt Wins Peace Prize

Although *Theodore Roosevelt* had a tough-guy image, he also worked hard for peace. In 1906 he became the first American to win the Nobel Peace Prize. He won this award for negotiating peace between Russia and Japan, who had been fighting for two years over land in Manchuria, China.

The Philippines

The Philippines became a U.S. territory after the *Spanish-American War* (see pp. 80-81). The *Tydings-McDuffie Act* of 1934 offered the Philippines independence after a period of preparation. Japan invaded the Philippines at the start of *World War II* (see p. 106). In 1946, after the U.S. defeat of Japan in World War II, the Philippines became independent.

TWENTIETH CENTURY— THE UNITED STATES AS WORLD LEADER

1 World War I (1914-1918)

World War I was the first war that involved countries from all over the world. Although the war started in 1914, the United States did not enter the war until 1917. When it was over, the boundaries of several European countries had changed. Although it was described as a "war to end all wars," World War I set the stage for another world war among many of the same nations (see pp. 98-107).

The *Allies* fought against the *Central (Axis) Powers* in World War I.

ALLIES	CENTRAL POWERS
Belgium	Germany
Great Britain	Austria-Hungary
France	Bulgaria
Italy (from 1915)	The Ottoman Empire
Japan	(Turkey)
most of North Africa	
Portugal	
Romania	
Russia	
United States (from 1917)	

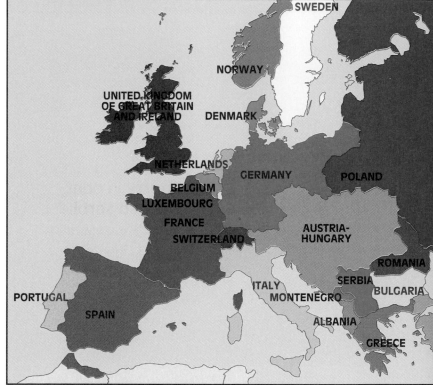

Europe before World War I

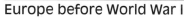

World War I begins in Europe — 1914

Germans sink the *Lusitania* — 1915

United States enters World War I — 1917

World War I ends — 1918

Nineteenth Amendment gives women the right to vote — 1920

Stock market crashes on October 29 — 1929

Franklin Roosevelt elected President — 1932

Adolph Hitler becomes German chancellor — 1933

Congress passes Social Security Act — 1935

World War II begins — 1939

Japan bombs Pearl Harbor

United States declares war on Japan, and enters World War II — 1941

United States drops atomic bomb on Hiroshima and Nagasaki, Japan

World War II ends.

United Nations is founded — 1945

84

> Propaganda *is information that emphasizes only one side of a story. It is often used in wartime.*

Causes of World War I

1 The industrial countries of Europe were very competitive. Some had large world empires. Their leaders wanted to increase the size of these empires.

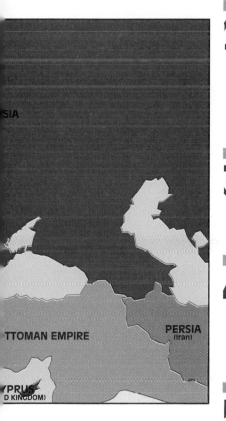

2 To protect themselves from each other, countries formed alliances. These alliances said that if one nation was attacked, the other nations would defend it. France, Russia, and Great Britain had an alliance called the Triple Entente. Germany, Austria-Hungary, and Italy signed the Triple Alliance.

3 The war was triggered by the assassination of the Austrian Archduke Franz Ferdinand in Sarajevo, Serbia, a small country in Central Europe. In response, Austria-Hungary attacked Serbia.

4 The alliances brought many countries into the war. Russia came to the aid of Serbia. Germany then declared war on Russia. France declared war on Germany. Germany attacked Belgium. Britain entered the war to help Belgium and France.

5 Many Czechs, Slovaks, and other Slavic peoples, seeking freedom from Austria-Hungary, fought for the Allies.

Reasons for Entering World War I

When war broke out in Europe, the United States declared that it would remain neutral, or not take sides. Both sides created a great deal of propaganda to persuade Americans that the other side was wrong.

The United States began to turn against Germany after German submarines, called ***U-boats***, sank the *Lusitania*, an unarmed British passenger ship, killing almost 1200 people, including more than 100 American passengers. The United States said the sinking of the *Lusitania* went against the international law that says that all seas are neutral territory. German U-boats also sank several unarmed American commercial ships. The continued sinking of American ships eventually led President ***Woodrow Wilson*** to ask Congress to declare war on Germany in 1917.

Results of World War I

The Treaty of Versailles, which ended the war, made the following conditions:

1 Germany was forced to give up territory and colonies to France, Belgium, Denmark, and Poland.

2 To prevent Germany from starting another war, the size of its army was reduced. It was forbidden to have submarines and aircraft.

3 Germany accepted responsibility for starting the war and was penalized $33 million in damages to other nations.

4 The League of Nations was formed (see p. 91).

5 Territories, such as Palestine (now Israel), were made protectorates (put under the protection) of Great Britain and other Allied countries.

The Treaty of Versailles severely punished Germany. Even though Germany never paid all the thirty-three million dollars, the penalties damaged its already weakened economy. Historians now think that the loss of pride and economic hardship led Germans to elect *Adolf Hitler* (see p. 98). The harshness of the Treaty of Versailles was a major cause of World War II.

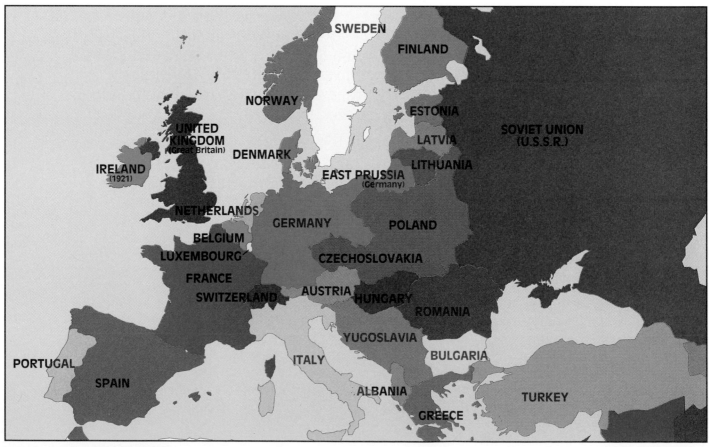

Europe after World War I

World War I was one of the bloodiest and most destructive wars in world history. New technology—poisonous gases, fighter planes, machine guns, grenades, and tanks—made warfare more horrible than people had ever imagined.

Much of the war was fought in trenches—long, narrow ditches dug by soldiers to hide in. They zigzagged all along the **Western Front**, the battle line that divided the Allied and Central powers (see p. 84). The Western Front was 450 miles long and ran through Belgium and France to Switzerland.

Barbed wire was stretched along the top of the trenches. Between the two sides was a deadly "no man's land." The moment soldiers entered it, they could be instantly killed by enemy fire. Poisonous gases, like mustard gas, spread easily throughout the trenches and made life even more miserable. "Inside the gas mask my head booms and roars," wrote one soldier. "I feel I am suffocating."

Millions of soldiers were killed in the trenches, trying to advance the battle lines just a few feet. The battle of the Somme, fought in northern France, lasted from June to November of 1916. During those six months, more than a million men were killed. The Allies gained only seven square miles of territory.

World Leaders in World War I

Woodrow Wilson

Premier of France and Minister of War during World War I, *Georges Benjamin Clemenceau* was nicknamed "The Tiger" because of his aggressive style. He was seventy-six years old when the war ended.

Prime Minister of Britain from 1916 to 1922, *David Lloyd George* wanted to make sure that Germany lost its navy and its empire in World War I. He pressed for harsh terms in the treaty that ended the war.

A grandson of Queen Victoria of England, Kaiser (King) *Wilhelm II* ruled Germany from 1888 to 1918. He fled to Holland to avoid capture after Germany was defeated.

Nicholas II was the last Czar (King) of Russia. He was forced from the throne in 1917 when the war was not going well for Russia. He and his family were murdered in 1918 by Bolsheviks, a revolutionary party.

The 28th President of the United States, *Woodrow Wilson* did his best to keep the United States out of World War I. When the war was over, he promoted the *League of Nations* (see p. 91) to help to solve disputes peacefully between countries.

1917

January	Britain enters Palestine
February	Germany declares unrestricted U-boat warfare and sinks five American ships
March 12	Russian Revolution begins
April 6	United States declares war on Germany
April 9	Battle of Arras, France
April 10	Canadians capture Vimy Ridge, France
April 16–May 9	French attack on Second Battle of Aisne River, France
May 25	Daylight bombing raids on Britain begin
June 7	British attack Messines Ridge, Belgium
July 31–November 6	Third Battle of Ypres–British against Germans
November 6-7	Canadians capture Passchendaele and end Battle of Ypres; Bolshevik revolution begins in Russia
November 20	Battle of Cambrai — British use large number of tanks to win
December 9	British capture Jerusalem in Middle East; Armistice (a cease-fire before signing a peace treaty) between Romania and Central Powers
December 15	Armistice between Russia and Central Powers

1918

January 8	President Woodrow Wilson proposes fourteen-point Peace Plan
April 9	Germans begin attack in northern France
May 27-30	Germans break Allied line on the Marne River
August 8	Allies rout Germans at Battle of Amiens
September 26	Final Allied attack begins
October 1	British capture Damascus, Syria
October 30	Battle of Vittorio Veneto, Italy — Italy defeats Austria-Hungary; Turkey signs Armistice
November 3	Austria-Hungary signs Armistice
November 9	Revolution in Berlin, Germany; Kaiser Wilhelm II gives up the throne, and Germany becomes a republic
November 11	Germany signs Armistice; War on Western Front ends

United States casualties: 323,000 (dead and wounded)
Total world casualties: about 10 million dead and about 20 million wounded

2 The League of Nations

President **Woodrow Wilson** proposed the **League of Nations** as a means of keeping peace among the nations of the world. The league was established in January 1920 after World War I, but fell apart at the start of World War II. It was officially dissolved in April 1946, when the United Nations began operations (see pp. 108-109).

Despite Wilson's leading role in founding the League, the United States never joined. At that time, there was a strong movement in U.S. foreign policy called isolationism. **Isolationism** meant not getting involved in the quarrels of other nations.

In its early years, the League of Nations settled some disputes between nations. In some cases, it even prevented war. But still it failed.

Reasons for Failure of the League of Nations

1 The League originally included every major nation except the United States. The Soviet Union joined in 1934, but was kicked out later. Germany and Japan withdrew in 1933.

2 Most major decisions required that all countries agree, which rarely happened.

3 The League had no power to tax its members. There was no way to raise money for its programs.

4 The League could not raise an army to enforce its decisions.

5 The League was unable to prevent: Japan from invading Manchuria (on the Asian mainland); Italy from conquering Ethiopia (in Africa); the Chaco War between Bolivia and Paraguay.

3 Women Win the Vote

Until 1920, women were not allowed to vote in U.S. Presidential elections. Their rights to enter into legal contracts, control money, and inherit or own property were limited. They were denied almost all business, professional, and educational opportunities. Most colleges did not even admit women.

Many American women sought to gain *equal rights* with men. Before the Civil War (see pp. 59-65), women were very active in the abolitionist movement to end slavery (see p. 54). They considered the struggle of African Americans to gain freedom and rights much like their own. In 1848, *Elizabeth Cady Stanton* and *Lucretia Coffin Mott* organized the first Women's Rights Convention in Seneca Falls, New York. The women and men who attended called for equal rights for women in education, voting, ownership of property, and other areas.

After the Civil War, women were disappointed that the vote was given only to African-American men. Some called for an amendment to the Constitution to grant women *suffrage*, or the right to vote. Over the following decades, a dozen states and territories allowed women to vote in elections within their borders. But the struggle for national suffrage took fifty-five more years. The 19th Amendment finally guaranteed this right in 1920.

▶ *Women's rights were an issue in the 1800s, and the call for these rights gained a louder voice as the years went by. As early as 1852, Matilda Joslyn Gage spoke these words at the Women's Rights Convention: "Self-reliance is one of the first lessons to be taught to our daughters; they should be educated with our sons and equally with them taught to look forward to some independent means of support."*

Men, women, and children joined forces to demonstrate for women's suffrage.

Some Women in the SUFFRAGE MOVEMENT

Although the 19th Amendment was ratified in 1920—fourteen years after her death—the amendment is known as the **Susan B. Anthony** amendment in honor of this woman's tireless efforts for women's rights and suffrage. From 1850, Anthony and **Elizabeth Cady Stanton** joined forces and became lifelong friends in a battle, fought in lecture halls and on printed pages, to improve the quality of life for women in the United States.

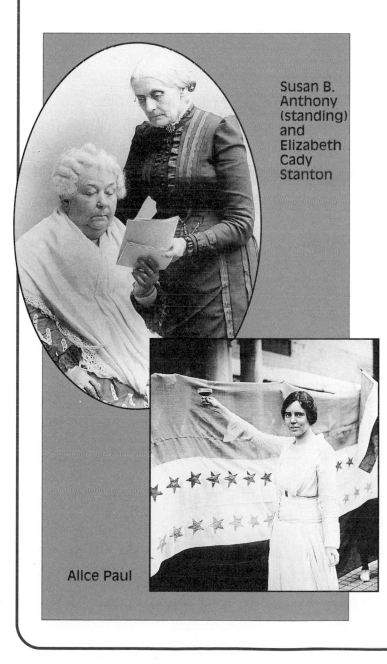

Susan B. Anthony (standing) and Elizabeth Cady Stanton

Alice Paul

A suffragist leader in the early 20th century, **Carrie Chapman Catt** was president of the National American Woman Suffrage Association. Catt tried to influence male politicians through reason and, later, by supporting **World War I** (see pp. 84-90).

A teacher and Quaker minister who became a speaker for the rights of women and labor and the abolition of slavery, **Lucretia Coffin Mott** helped organize the first Women's Rights Convention in the United States in Seneca Falls, New York.

A leader at the same time as **Carrie Chapman Catt**, **Alice Paul** founded the National Women's Party. This organization focused public attention on women's suffrage by embarrassing politicians through marches, picketing, and hunger strikes. After the Constitution was amended to allow women to vote, she campaigned for an equal rights amendment.

Representative **Jeannette Rankin** of Montana was the first woman to be elected to Congress in 1916. She was the only person to vote against entry into both World Wars I and II. Defeated in 1918, she ran again in 1940 and was reelected.

Elizabeth Cady Stanton was one of the first women's rights activists. The daughter of a lawyer, she dedicated her life from an early age to the struggle for women's rights. With **Lucretia Mott**, she organized the first Women's Rights Convention. In 1872, Stanton asked the Senate Judiciary Committee: "We have declared in favor of a government of the people, for the people, and by the people. Why not begin the experiment?"

Lucy Stone was one of the most popular suffragettes, as well as an **abolitionist** (see p. 54). She was an excellent speaker, and toured the nation, giving talks and passing out petitions. In 1855, she married **Henry Blackwell**, but insisted on keeping her name. She and her husband drew up a marriage contract of equal partnership.

4 The 1920s

After World War I, business in the United States continued to grow. The economy was strong. People had money because they could get credit (buy now and pay later). Many people played the stock market and invested in get-rich-quick schemes. Across the nation, people had more time to relax. Radio and the movies kept them entertained. Art, music, and literature thrived. The period was marked by high living and fun, and so came to be called the *Roaring Twenties*.

Life even got better, briefly, for some African Americans. In New York's Harlem, black artists and writers won recognition and good pay. This period of cultural rebirth is called the *Harlem Renaissance*. The Harlem Renaissance included musicians *Duke Ellington, Cab Calloway*, and singer *Marian Anderson.* Writers included the poet *Langston Hughes* and the novelist *Zora Neale Hurston*, who wrote with awareness and pride about the African-American experience.

But the big boom did not last. Many companies made more products than people could buy. In 1929, the values of company stocks crashed, or fell suddenly. The Roaring Twenties were over and the Great Depression began (see pp. 95-97).

Many new pastimes were enjoyed during the Roaring Twenties. Among the fads was a dance called the Charleston.

5 The Great Depression

The *Stock Market Crash of 1929* was devastating. Businesses went *bankrupt*, which meant they lost all their money and were unable to pay their debts. Over 5,000 banks failed in the next two years—seemingly overnight. More than twelve million people — one out of three workers — lost their jobs. Many people who still had jobs were forced to work for much less pay. Some earned as little as ten cents an hour.

The Crash marks the starting point of the *Great Depression*, an era of hardship and sadness quite unlike the Roaring Twenties (see p. 94). There were no government programs like unemployment, welfare, or social security to help people who were out of work. Many people lost their entire life savings in the course of a single day.

Causes of the Great Depression

1 The business boom of the 1920s made people overly confident. They invested their money in risky stocks and deals.

2 Banks made careless loans. When people could not pay them back, the banks failed.

3 Businesses produced more goods than they could sell.

4 Machines replaced human workers in many factory jobs.

5 Many people borrowed money they couldn't repay.

6 People had invested most of their money in stocks. When stock prices crashed, they lost all their savings.

By 1932, twelve million people in the United States were jobless. While jobs were scarce, bread lines were common.

FDR and the New Deal

Franklin Delano Roosevelt (FDR) was elected President in 1932 at the depth of the Great Depression. He had been elected on his promise to get the economy back on its feet. In 1933, after only a few weeks in office, FDR proposed a plan called the *New Deal*. It included dozens of new programs designed to help the nation through its economic crisis and put people back to work. Most of FDR's programs became law.

The New Deal offered new federal programs to improve the economy and to help those in need. FDR also began a series of radio talks called the *fireside chats*. He spoke on the air about conditions in the nation and what the government was doing about them. These informal talks made people feel more confident and hopeful.

By 1939, business had improved, but there were still about nine million people who had not been put back to work. The economy did not fully recover until the U.S. entered *World War II* (see pp. 98-107).

Franklin
Delano
Roosevelt

Major New Deal Acts and Agencies

1 Federal Emergency Relief Administration (FERA): Provided funds for local and state relief organizations.

2 Social Security Act: Gave benefits to the elderly and orphaned and to people injured in industrial accidents.

3 Agricultural Adjustment Act (AAA): Gave farmers money to make up for the government's request that they bring fewer crops to market.

4 Works Progress Administration (WPA): Provided government funds for constructing buildings and to hire writers and artists.

5 Tennessee Valley Authority (TVA): Provided funds to develop the Tennessee River valley.

6 National Industry Recovery Act (NIRA): Created work codes and industry safety regulations.

7 Civilian Conservation Corps (CCC): Gave twenty-five million young men work in environmental improvement projects.

8 Farm Security Administration (FSA): Lent money to sharecroppers and tenant farmers to help them buy their own land.

9 National Labor Relations Board (NLRB): Guaranteed workers the right to join labor unions and call strikes.

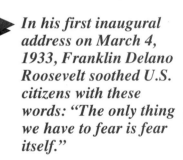

In his first inaugural address on March 4, 1933, Franklin Delano Roosevelt soothed U.S. citizens with these words: "The only thing we have to fear is fear itself."

More People from the Depression and the New Deal

Mary McLeod Bethune spent her life trying to improve the lives of African Americans through education. She was appointed director of Negro Affairs for the National Youth Administration in 1935. She organized high-level African Americans, known as the ***Black Cabinet***, to offer advice on New Deal programs (see p. 96). Bethune started Bethune-Cookman College in Florida.

The president of the United Mine Workers, ***John L. Lewis*** was an organizer of the Congress of Industrial Organizations (see p. 75). In 1943, he led a strike of 450,000 coal miners when the National War Labor Board refused to approve a raise. Eventually, the government, Lewis, and the mine operators agreed on a raise.

Democratic Senator ***Huey Long*** of Louisiana was a major opponent of Roosevelt's ***New Deal*** (see p. 75). A spell-binding speaker with a vast following of workers, he blamed the rich for the nation's troubles. He proposed that all incomes over five million dollars be taken away and given to the less fortunate. But there were many charges that Long misused public money, and he made many enemies. In 1935, he was assassinated.

Frances Perkins

The first woman cabinet member, ***Frances Perkins*** was Franklin Delano Roosevelt's Secretary of Labor. She started her career working with ***Jane Addams*** (see p. 77) in Chicago. She spent her life working to improve conditions for American workers, and helped influence Congress to pass the Social Security Act (see p. 96).

The wife of ***Franklin Delano Roosevelt, Eleanor Roosevelt*** was one of America's most popular First Ladies. She was involved in political issues, wrote magazine articles, and gave radio talks. She was interested in improving conditions for the poor, elderly, and for African Americans. Roosevelt said, "We cannot exist as a little island of well-being in a world where two-thirds of the people go to bed hungry every night."

Republican Senator ***Robert Taft*** of Ohio opposed the New Deal (see p. 96) protections for workers and trade unions. Believing that workers had too much influence, he introduced the ***Taft-Hartley Act*** in 1947, which gave the government and management new powers to break strikes. President ***Harry S Truman*** vetoed the bill, but Congress passed it over his veto.

A retired physician, ***Francis E. Townsend*** started a movement in 1933 by expressing the frustrations of many Americans with the slow pace of recovery under the New Deal (see p. 96). Townsend proposed that every American man be encouraged to retire at age sixty and given a sum of money each month of his retirement. He thought this would free up jobs and encourage spending. Today, retirement is common in many companies for workers aged sixty and over.

6 World War II (1939-1945)

World War II was the result of Germany, Italy, and Japan's conquests of neighboring nations in the late 1930s. The *Allies*—Britain, France, and the United States—tried very hard to avoid war. Britain and France tried to negotiate with Germany, but Germany broke its promises. Eventually, war broke out in Europe as Nazi Germany, led by *Adolf Hitler*, conquered one nation after another. The *Nazis* were the ruling German political party during Hitler's time in power.

Many U.S. citizens did not want to become involved in World War II. They felt it was a European matter. These people were called *Isolationists*, because they wanted to "isolate" the United States from involvement in a foreign war. Others believed strongly that the United States should enter at once to help Britain and to defeat Hitler.

The United States debated what to do until the end of 1941. On December 7, 1941, Japan bombed the U.S. naval base at Pearl Harbor, Hawaii. The United States was united in its anger. It declared war on Japan and entered the war on the side of the Allies.

World War II was the first war in which the airplane played an important role, and air strikes were a major part of strategy. Many kinds of advanced technology were put to use during the war — radar, guided missiles, jet-propelled planes, and the atomic bomb.

World War II lasted for six years and was fought on many fronts in Europe, Asia, the Islands of the Pacific, and Africa. It ended in the total defeat of Germany and Japan and established the United States as a world leader. It was also the beginning of a rivalry between the United States and the Union of Soviet Socialist Republics (or Soviet Union), the enormous nation built by the Russians.

Seventy million soldiers from forty countries were involved in World War II, and fighting occurred on six continents and all oceans.

THE ALLIES	THE AXIS
Great Britain (with its empire, including Canada and India)	Germany
	Italy
China	Japan
France	Soviet Union (until 1941)
Soviet Union (from 1941)	
United States (from 1941)	

Sherman tank

German fighter planes

Causes of World War II

1 Dictators in Germany, Japan, and Italy promoted a fanatical national pride. They also took over the government and installed themselves as the sole heads of state. To support their regime they created powerful police networks that enforced their ideas of government.

2 The Treaty of Versailles (see p. 86) left Germany poor and its national pride injured.

3 The Axis powers wanted to conquer their neighbors. Japan wanted a "New Order" in Asia; Italy wanted to rule much of Africa; and Germany wanted to rule Europe. Each invaded other countries and replaced their governments with military dictatorships.

U.S. general infantry soldier

The Holocaust

Nazi Germany's War Against the European Jews

In one of the worst and most tragic chapters of World War II, Nazis in Germany organized the murder of millions of Jews and other people. This dark period is known as the ***Holocaust***. (A *holocaust* is a disaster that wipes out life.) The Holocaust was not a dispute over land, nor was it a power struggle. It was a systematic attempt to exterminate all Jews simply because they were Jews.

Before World War II, ***Adolf Hitler*** dreamed of a world ruled by white people he called Aryans. He built many walled prisons called ***concentration camps*** in Germany and Poland. Some were work camps where prisoners made supplies for the German army. Others were death factories. Hitler sent Jews and anyone who opposed his rule to these concentration camps.

Hitler was determined to eliminate the Jews, the biggest threat, he thought, to his Aryan supremacy. He killed over six million, a full forty percent of the world's Jewish population. Other groups, including Gypsies, the disabled, homosexuals, and political opponents of the Nazis, also became targets. Five million people from these groups lost their lives. Never before had organized murder taken place on such a horrifying scale.

In Nazi concentration camps, prisoners lived in cramped quarters with no personal possessions, except for the clothes on their backs and the dish issued them for food, if food was provided at all.

Results of World War II

1 World War II was the most expensive war in history. It cost more than one trillion dollars and left whole cities in ruin. Many countries faced hard economic times as a result.

2 Millions of people in Europe and Asia lost their homes. Some were unable even to return to their home countries. They needed help to start new lives.

3 Japan wrote a new constitution and formed a more democratic government.

4 Germany was divided into four parts, as was its capital, Berlin. West Germany became an independent democracy in 1949 when the French, British, and U.S. zones were united (the same three Berlin zones were united at this time as well). East Germany became a communist country closely watched by the Soviet Union. (The two Germanys were reunited in 1990.)

5 The United States and the Soviet Union became the chief world powers, and their differences led to the Cold War (see p. 109), which lasted for the next forty years.

6 The Soviet Union dominated those countries in Eastern Europe that its troops had liberated from the Axis powers.

Two Famous Scientists

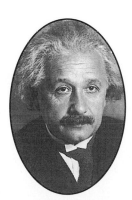

Albert Einstein

Albert Einstein was one of the world's greatest physicists. A Jew born in Germany, he moved to the United States in 1932 when the Nazi Party came to power. In 1940, he wrote a famous letter to President *Franklin Delano Roosevelt* which warned of the danger that Germany might develop an atomic bomb first. This warning led to the *Manhattan Project,* the top-secret atomic bomb research.

Robert Oppenheimer was the U.S. physicist who led the Manhattan Project, which developed the world's first atomic bomb. After the bomb was used on *Hiroshima* and *Nagasaki* in Japan, Oppenheimer became concerned about future uses of nuclear weapons. He opposed the development of a more advanced weapon, the hydrogen bomb.

Robert Oppenheimer

Neville Chamberlain

Winston Churchill

Dwight D. Eisenhower

Adolf Hitler

Douglas MacArthur

Prime Minister of Britain at the beginning of World War II, *Neville Chamberlain* was sure that *Adolf Hitler* could be satisfied by giving him more territory. In 1938, he attended a conference with Hitler, *Benito Mussolini,* and *Edouard Daladier* of France, where he agreed to give Hitler part of Czechoslovakia. Chamberlain was replaced by *Winston Churchill*, who favored taking a strong stand against Hitler.

Winston Churchill was named Prime Minister of Britain in 1940. He was an inspiring speaker, writer, and statesman. His courageous leadership and defiant speeches kept British morale high during the worst days of the war. In 1953, he won the Nobel Prize for literature for his memoirs.

The Supreme Commander of the Allied Forces, American General *Dwight D. Eisenhower* organized the massive Allied invasion of the French coast on *D-day* in 1944. In 1952 and 1956, he was elected President of the United States.

Adolf Hitler was an unsuccessful artist before he joined the National Socialist Workers' Party, known as the Nazis. Through his skill in propaganda and his use of terror he became the *Führer*, or leader, of Germany. His conquest of surrounding countries set off World War II, and his anti-semitic beliefs led to the Holocaust (see p. 100).

General *Douglas MacArthur* was commander of the U.S. forces in the Pacific during World War II. A proud man, MacArthur was fired later by President *Harry S Truman* for failing to follow orders during the Korean War (see p. 110).

Benito Mussolini

Franklin Delano Roosevelt

Josef Stalin

Hideki Tojo

Harry S Truman

During the 1920s, **Benito Mussolini** rose to power as dictator in Italy. He was head of the Fascist Party and wanted to build an Italian empire. He invaded the African nation of Ethiopia in 1935, and took over Albania in Eastern Europe in 1939. The Allies captured him when they moved into Italy, but the Germans rescued him. He was captured again in 1945 and shot.

The only President to be elected to four terms, **Franklin Delano Roosevelt** served during two great crises in American history— the Great Depression (see pp. 95-97) and World War II— while partially paralyzed by polio. He died on April 12, 1945, three weeks before Germany surrendered.

Josef Stalin was a Russian revolutionary who fought against the Czar **Nicholas II** of Russia and eventually became dictator of the Soviet Union. He took the name Stalin, which means "steel" in Russian. A ruthless person, he first tried to make a deal with **Adolf Hitler**, then joined the Allies when Hitler attacked the Soviet Union.

A key figure in the military government that ruled Japan after World War I, **Hideki Tojo** was dictator from 1941 to 1944. He wanted to build a New World Order in Asia, with Japan as its leader. At the end of the war, he was executed as a war criminal.

Vice President **Harry S Truman** became President when **Franklin Delano Roosevelt** died. It was his decision to drop two atomic bombs on Japan, which led to the Japanese surrender. After the war, he helped to rebuild the nations of Western Europe by offering billions of dollars in aid. This was named the **Marshall Plan** for then Secretary of State George Marshall.

Chronology of World War II

1939

March 15	**Hitler occupies Czechoslovakia and makes it part of Germany**
April 7	**Italy invades Albania and makes it part of Italy**
September 1	**Germany invades Poland**
September 3	**Britain declares war on Germany; France, Australia, New Zealand, and India follow**
September 10	**Canada declares war on Germany; U.S. remains neutral**
November 30	**Soviet Union invades Finland**

Lt. John F. Kennedy became a World War II hero for his efforts in saving all but two members of his crew when this boat was sunk in the Pacific by a Japanese destroyer.

1940

March 29	Soviet Union announces its neutrality
April 9	Germany invades Denmark and Norway
May 10	Germany attacks Belgium, The Netherlands, Luxembourg; Churchill becomes Prime Minister of Britain
June 5	Germany attacks France
June 10	Italy declares war on Britain and France; Canada declares war on Italy
June 14	Germans enter Paris
June 18	Charles de Gaulle, leader of the French Resistance, broadcasts from London for "Free France"
June 22	France surrenders to Germany
July 10	Battle of Britain begins — Britain wins in October
August 5	Italy attacks Allies in Africa
September 7	Germans begin "Blitz" bombing of London
September 27	Germany, Italy, and Japan sign Axis of Powers pact
December 9	Allies begin African attack against Italy

1941

March 1	Bulgaria joins Axis
March 25	Yugoslavia signs pact with Germany; its army resists
March 28	Battle of Cape Matapan
April 6	Germany invades Yugoslavia and Greece
May 24	Germany's ship Bismarck sinks British Hood
May 27	Bismarck sunk
June 22	Germany invades Soviet Union
September 18-19	Germany captures Kiev and Poltava, Russia
October 20	Germany attacks Moscow, Russia
November 18	Britain begins Western Desert Campaign in Africa
December 7	Japan bombs Pearl Harbor, Hawaii
December 8-11	Japan invades Thailand which joins Axis; United States, Britain, and Canada declare war on Japan; China declares war on the Axis; Germany and Italy declare war on the United States
December 25	Japan captures Hong Kong

1942

January 2	Japan occupies Manila, the Philippines
February 15	Japan captures Singapore
February 27	Battle of Java Sea begins in the South Pacific
March 11	General MacArthur leaves the Philippines, vowing "I shall return"
April 9	The Philippines surrenders to Japan
April 30	Japan captures Burma
May 4-8	Battle of Coral Sea near Australia
May 11	Japan invades China
May 30	Britain launches bomber raid on Cologne, Germany
June 4-6	Allies win Battle of Midway in the South Pacific
June 19	Roosevelt and Churchill meet in the United States
August 7	U.S. Marines land on Guadalcanal in the Solomon Islands
August 15	General Bernard Montgomery named commander of British troops in Middle East
August 25	Five-month German attack on Stalingrad begins
October 11	Battle of Cape Esperance near Guadalcanal—U.S. defeats Japanese
October 23-November 4	Battle of El Alamein, Egypt; Axis retreats
November 8	Allied troops land in Algeria and Morocco

1943

January 27	United States bombs Wilhelmshaven, Germany
February 2	Germans surrender at Stalingrad, Russia (turning point of war in favor of Allies)
February 8-16	Russians recapture Kursk and Kharkov, Russia
March 14	Germans recapture Kharkov
May 12	Axis troops in North Africa surrender
July 10	Invasion of Italy begins
July 25	Mussolini arrested and imprisoned
September 10	Germans occupy Rome, Italy
September 12	Mussolini rescued by Germans
October 1	Allies capture Naples, Italy
November 22	Allies capture Tarawa Island in the Pacific

1944

January 5	Allies attack northern Italy
March 24	U.S. victory in Solomon Islands
May 13	Allies get through German line on way to Rome, Italy
June 4	Allies recapture Rome
June 6	D-day — Allies invade Normandy, France
June 19-20	U.S. wins decisive air and naval victory in the Philippine Sea
June 27	Allies capture Cherbourg, France
July 17	Soviet troops enter Poland
July 18	Japanese Prime Minister Tojo resigns
July 20	German officers' attempt to assassinate Hitler fails
August	U.S. Marines occupy Guam and Tinian in the Pacific
August 25	Paris, France, is liberated by Allies
September 3-4	Allies liberate Brussels, Belgium, and Antwerp, Belgium
October 20	MacArthur returns to the Philippines
October 23-26	Battle of Leyte Gulf in the Pacific
December 16	Battle of the Bulge begins in Belgium and Luxembourg

1945

January 28	Battle of the Bulge ends
February 24	United States recaptures Manila, the Philippines
March 16	U.S. Marines capture Iwo Jima in Pacific
April 12	President Franklin Roosevelt dies; Harry Truman becomes President
April 13	Russia occupies Vienna, Austria
April 20	United States captures Nuremberg, Germany
April 25	Soviet forces encircle Berlin
April 28	Mussolini captured and killed by Italian resistance
April 29	German troops surrender in Italy
April 30	Hitler kills himself
May 2	Russians capture Berlin, Germany; German forces surrender in Italy
May 7	Germany surrenders
June 22	United States captures Okinawa in Pacific
August 6	United States drops atomic bomb on Hiroshima, Japan
August 9	United States drops atomic bomb on Nagasaki, Japan
September 2	Japan signs surrender

United States battle deaths: 300,000
Total world casualties: fifty-four million
military and civilian people dead; thirty-
four million wounded

7 The United Nations

The United Nations was founded in 1945 to maintain world peace and security. U.S. President *Franklin Roosevelt,* British Prime Minister *Winston Churchill,* and Soviet dictator *Josef Stalin* worked together to form this new organization. Congress approved U.S. membership in the United Nations. After World War II, more members of Congress were convinced that international cooperation might prevent future wars. The United Nations has its headquarters in New York City.

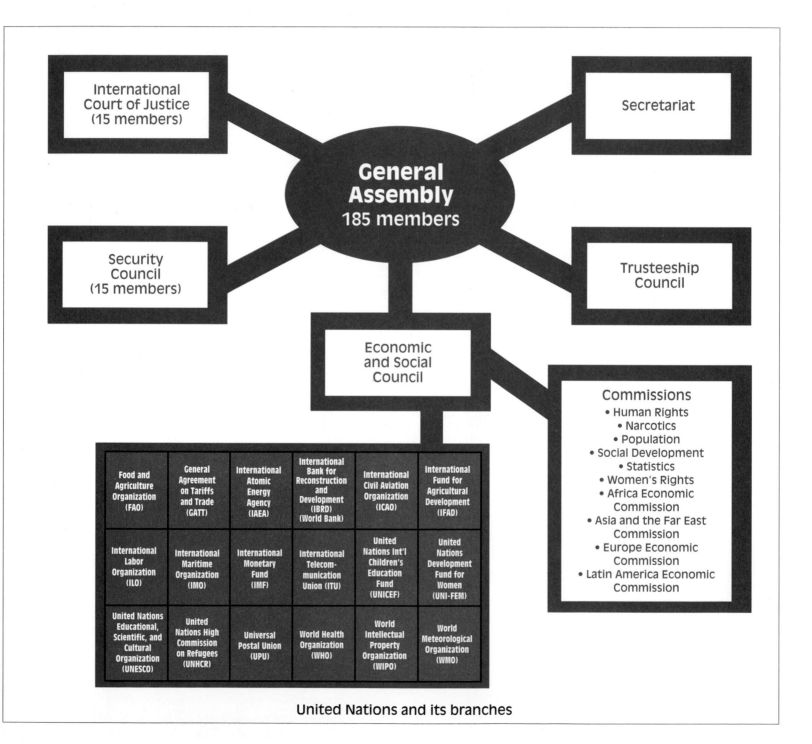

United Nations and its branches

Organization of the United Nations

The *General Assembly* is made up of all the members of the United Nations. Each member has one vote. The General Assembly can make recommendations, but cannot give orders to act militarily.

The *Security Council* is made up of fifteen members. There are five permanent members—the United States, Britain, France, Russia, and the People's Republic of China. The other ten members are elected to two-year terms. Only the Security Council can order the United Nations to take action. To do this, nine of the fifteen members must vote for action. All five permanent members must also vote in favor of the action. Any one of the permanent members can veto, or reject, a call for action.

The *International Court of Justice*, which meets at the Hague in the Netherlands, is made up of fifteen judges who decide cases by majority vote. When nations submit their cases to the court, they agree to accept its decision.

The *Secretariat* consists of the *Secretary General* and his or her staff. They are responsible for running the United Nations. The Secretary General is appointed by the General Assembly for a five-year term.

The Cold War

The Cold War was a war of words, not guns. It was a struggle between the democratic nations of the West—such as the United States, Great Britain, and France—and the nations allied with the former Soviet Union.

The Soviet Union was ruled by a communist dictatorship in which all its people were to share in the nation's wealth and government. In fact, dictators and the Communist Party tightly controlled every part of the Soviet people's lives. Both the Soviet Union and United States wanted to protect their interests and gain allies around the world. The United States and its allies in the *North Atlantic Treaty Organization* (NATO) resisted the communists. The Soviets responded by forming the *Warsaw Pact* with their allies.

As each side tried to win over other countries, conflicts flared up all over the world. Both the United States and the Soviet Union built many nuclear weapons, which they pointed at each other. The Cold War lasted from the end of World War II until 1989, when the Berlin Wall was torn down and Soviet Communism ended (see p. 112).

APPENDIX A
EVENTS SINCE WORLD WAR II

1945: The *Cold War* begins (see p. 109). Soviet troops remain in the countries they freed from the Germans, including Poland, Hungary, Czechoslovakia, and Bulgaria. In 1945, Germany and its capital, Berlin, are split into four zones.

1946: British Prime Minister *Winston Churchill* declares, "An iron curtain has descended across the continent (Europe)." The term *iron curtain* becomes a popular way to describe the split between communist Eastern Europe and democratic Western Europe.
The Soviet Union begins supporting governments in Eastern Europe which are friendly toward the Soviets.

1948-1949: Soviet dictator *Josef Stalin* blockades traffic around West Berlin, which lies within East Germany.
American planes fly supplies to Germans stranded in West Berlin in what becomes known as the *Berlin Airlift.*

1949: *North Atlantic Treaty Organization* (NATO), composed of Western democracies, is formed. By 1954, members include the United States, Canada, Iceland, Norway, Britain, the Netherlands, Denmark, Belgium, France, Luxembourg, Portugal, Italy, Greece, and Turkey. West Germany will join in 1955, and Spain in 1982.
Soviets explode an atomic bomb.

1950: War breaks out in *Korea* between the communist North and the non-communist South.
U.S. economic aid to South Vietnam, Laos, and Cambodia in Southeast Asia begins.

1950-1954: U.S. Senator *Joseph McCarthy* accuses many government workers and prominent Americans of being Communists.

1953: Former Allied Supreme Commander *Dwight D. Eisenhower* becomes President. *Korean War* ends.

1954: In *Brown vs. Board of Education,* the U.S. Supreme Court rules that segregation of public schools by race violates the Constitution.
Dr. *Jonas Salk* introduces vaccine to immunize people against polio, a disease that had crippled tens of thousands of people.

1955: The *Warsaw Pact,* composed of communist dictatorships, is formed in response to NATO. Members are the Soviet Union, Albania, Bulgaria, Czechoslovakia, East Germany, Hungary, Poland, and Romania.

1956: *Martin Luther King, Jr.*, rises as leader of the nonviolent civil rights movement in the United States.

1957: Soviet Union launches the first satellite, *Sputnik,* into outer space.

1959: First two U.S. soldiers are killed in Vietnam.

1960: *John F. Kennedy* elected president. He calls his new program for the United States *The New Frontier*, and says in his inaugural address: "Ask not what your country can do for you—ask what you can do for your country."

1961: Communists build a heavily guarded barrier across the city of Berlin—the *Berlin Wall*—to prevent East German citizens from fleeing to the West. *Bay of Pigs* invasion by the United States fails to free the Caribbean island of Cuba from dictator *Fidel Castro*.

1962: *Cuban Missile Crisis* occurs when the United States discovers that the Soviet Union has put nuclear missiles in Cuba. The Soviets agree to remove the weapons. *Cesar Chavez* founds *National Farm Workers Association* in California to improve conditions for migrant farm laborers.

1963: President Kennedy assassinated; *Lyndon B. Johnson* becomes President. Martin Luther King, Jr. delivers speech: "I have a dream...that my four little children will one day live in a nation where they will not be judged by the color of their skin but by the content of their character."

1964: President Johnson elected to a full term. He gets Congress to pass a resolution to send thousands of U.S. troops to *Vietnam*.

1966: *National Organization for Women* (NOW) founded.

1968: Both *Martin Luther King, Jr.*, and Senator *Robert Kennedy*, brother of John F. Kennedy, are assassinated. *Richard M. Nixon* elected President.

1969: U.S. astronauts *Neil Armstrong* and *Edwin Aldrin* become the first humans to land on the moon. On a live television broadcast, Armstrong claims the achievement is: "One small step for a man, one giant leap for mankind." Anti-Vietnam War protesters hold their largest rally in Washington, D.C.

1970: Environmental Protection Agency (EPA) founded to set standards for clean air, water, and land.

1972: President Nixon visits China, the first visit by a U.S. President since its takeover by a communist government in 1949. *Watergate* break-in starts chain of events that ends the Nixon Presidency. Years of *detente* begin when communist and non-communist nations develop friendlier relations and sign several arms control treaties.

1973: Fighting stops in *Vietnam War*. United States has a severe shortage of oil and gas because oil-producing Arab nations, angered over U.S. support for Israel, stop selling oil to the United States. Supreme Court legalizes abortion in *Roe vs. Wade.*

1974: *Richard M. Nixon* resigns; *Gerald R. Ford* becomes President.

1976: *James Carter* elected President.

1978: President Carter hosts meeting between Egyptian President *Anwar Sadat* and Israeli Prime Minister *Menachem Begin* at Camp David, Maryland. The two agree to sign a peace treaty.

1979: Muslim Fundamentalists in Iran take fifty-three U.S. citizens hostage.

1980: *Ronald Reagan* elected President.

1981: *Sandra Day O'Connor* becomes first female Supreme Court justice. Hostages released in Iran.

1984: President Reagan elected to a second term. The United States enjoys a period of good business and prosperity, but U.S. debt also grows.

1985: *Mikhail Gorbachev* comes to power in the Soviet Union. Over a period of several years, Gorbachev introduces *perestroika* (restructuring) and *glasnost* (openness) in his country. These policies are welcomed in the United States because they mean that the *Cold War* may soon be over.

1987: Stock market plunges 508 points in one day. Some people worry that it may be like the Crash of 1929 (see p. 95), but no serious problems follow.

1988: *George Bush* elected President.

1989: Berlin Wall falls, signalling the end of the *Cold War*.

1989-1990: Communist dictatorships fall throughout Eastern Europe, now that it is clear *Mikhail Gorbachev* will not back them up by military force. The Soviet Union dissolves into many separate countries.

1990-1991: War breaks out in the Persian Gulf as Iraq invades Kuwait. The United States fights to keep Iraqi leader *Saddam Hussein* from succeeding. The U.S. invasion, begun in January and finished in April 1991, is called Desert Storm.

1992: *William Clinton* elected President.

1993: President Clinton signs the North American Free Trade Agreement (NAFTA) to end trade barriers among the United States, Canada, and Mexico, and the Brady Bill, regulating the sale of guns.

1994: Major earthquakes rock Los Angeles, California, killing 51. U.S. planes bomb Serbian targets in an effort to end civil war between Bosnians and Serbians. Congress votes for the Global Trade Alliance (GATT).

1995: Republicans become the majority in Congress for the first time since 1955. A federal office building in Oklahoma City, Oklahoma, is the target of a terrorist car bombing, which kills more than 200 people.

1996: The U.S. commits to leading a world wide ban on nuclear testing and signs START II, a nuclear arms pact.

APPENDIX B

1 American Government

The Preamble to the Constitution of the United States

We the people of the United States, in order to form a more perfect union, establish justice, insure domestic tranquility, provide for the common defense, promote the general welfare, and secure the blessings of liberty to ourselves and our posterity, do ordain and establish this Constitution for the United States of America.

The Preamble Explained

The Preamble is the *introduction* to the Constitution. It announces that people in the United States have to set up their own government to keep peace at home and to defend themselves against other countries, and that the government will do what needs to be done to provide freedom for all people.

The Constitution sets up a system in which a national, or *federal*, government is the strongest in the land, stronger than the state governments that created the Constitution. The United States is also called a *republic*, which means that it has no king or queen.

Powers of the Constitution

1 The Federal and State government share power

The Constitution provides for a federal system of government in which power is divided between the states and the federal government. The federal government is responsible for things the states cannot do, and states can do certain things the federal government cannot do. For example, only the federal government can make money, declare war, or control trade between the states. State governments control education, marriage, divorce, and form police forces. Both the federal and state governments can pass taxes, build roads, and try lawbreakers.

2 Representation of the people

A representative form of government has been set up in which voters elect representatives for Congress. These representatives make the laws. The number of representatives from any state in the House of Representatives, or lower house, is based on the population of each state. In the Senate, or upper house, each state has two Senators, regardless of its size or population.

3 Checks and Balances

The power of the federal government is shared by its three branches—*executive, legislative,* and *judicial.* Each of these branches has certain powers. The branches also have limited power to check each other. By separating the power among the three areas, no branch can become too powerful. This is called a system of *checks and balances*.

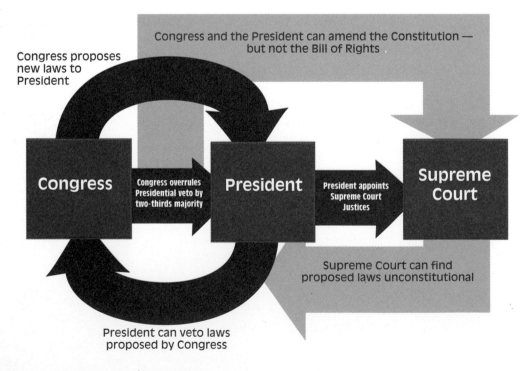

Congress proposes new laws to President

Congress and the President can amend the Constitution — but not the Bill of Rights

Congress — Congress overrules Presidential veto by two-thirds majority — **President** — President appoints Supreme Court Justices — **Supreme Court**

Supreme Court can find proposed laws unconstitutional

President can veto laws proposed by Congress

The system of checks and balances affects how legislation is passed and made law in the United States.

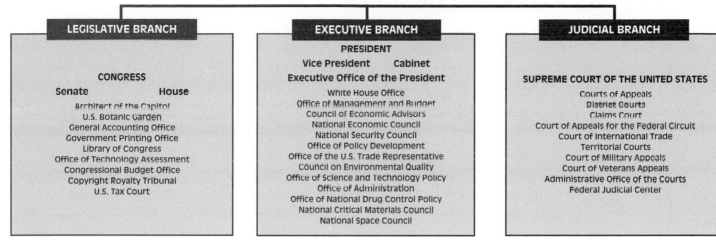

UNITED STATES GOVERNMENT

THE LEGISLATIVE BRANCH

The legislative branch, or Congress, is made up of the House of Representatives and the Senate. Congress makes the laws that govern all Americans. Laws must pass by a majority vote of both houses of Congress. The President can check the power of Congress by *vetoing*, or saying no to, a bill. If the President vetoes a bill, Congress can override the veto by a two-thirds vote of both the Senate and the House of Representatives.

Congress can also check the President by refusing to approve the appointment of a judge or cabinet member. It can also refuse to approve a budget, leaving the President without funds to govern. Congress also has the power to remove a President from office if he or she has committed serious wrongdoings. This is called *impeachment*. A trial is held and a two-thirds majority vote in the Senate is needed to remove a President.

THE JUDICIAL BRANCH

The judicial branch decides whether federal laws have been broken. It can also be asked to decide if laws passed by Congress and actions of the President are in agreement with the principles of the Constitution. If the Supreme Court decides a law or action goes against the principles of the Constitution, it is said to be *unconstitutional.* The law is dropped, or the President is forced to change the action. This is a powerful check over the legislative and executive branches.

All federal judges, including Supreme Court Justices, are appointed for life by the President. The Senate checks the judicial and executive branches by approving these appointments.

THE EXECUTIVE BRANCH

The executive branch sees that the laws made by Congress are carried out. The President is the head of this branch and is chosen by the *electoral college*. The electoral college is chosen by the voters in the country to vote for the various Presidential candidates (see p. 119). The President appoints the cabinet and many other officials. These appointments must have the approval of the Senate. This is a check of the legislative branch over the executive branch. The President also has the power to veto a bill that Congress has passed. This veto can be overridden by a two-thirds vote of the Senate and the House of Representatives.

Powers of the President

- The President is chief executive of the government. He or she sees that all laws passed by Congress are carried out. The President also sends to Congress the annual budget needed to run the government and proposals for raising money.

- As Commander-in-Chief of the Armed Forces, the President gives orders to the military services. The President may ask Congress to declare war and decides how to conduct war.

- The President must either sign or veto all bills passed by Congress.

- The President appoints all judges serving on the Supreme Court and other United States courts, ambassadors to foreign countries, cabinet members, and chief officers of the army, navy, and air force.

- The President directs foreign policy and makes treaties with foreign countries with the consent of the Senate.

Order of Power

If a President is unable to serve out his term, Presidential power is passed along in the following order:

1. President

2. Vice President

3. Speaker of the House of Representatives

4. President Pro Tempore of the Senate

5. Secretary of State

6. Secretary of the Treasury

7. Secretary of Defense

8. Attorney General

9. Secretary of the Interior

10. Secretary of Agriculture

11. Secretary of Commerce

Members of the President's Cabinet

Secretary of Agriculture
Secretary of Commerce
Secretary of Defense
Secretary of Education
Secretary of Energy
Secretary of Health and Human Services
Secretary of Housing and Urban Development
Secretary of the Interior
Attorney General
Secretary of Labor
Secretary of State (Foreign Affairs)
Secretary of Transportation
Secretary of the Treasury
Secretary of Veterans Affairs

Requirements for Federal Office

Requirements for President

1. Must be thirty-five years old.
2. Must be a citizen born in the United States.
3. Must have lived in the United States for fourteen consecutive years.
Term: Four years. May be re-elected once.

Requirements for Congress

Senator

1. Must be thirty years old.
2. Must have been a citizen for at least nine years.
3. Must be a resident of the state from which elected.
Term: Six years. One third of the Senate is elected every two years. The Vice President serves as the President of the Senate.

Representative

1. Must be at least twenty-five years old.
2. Must have been a citizen for at least seven years.
3. Must be a resident of the state from which elected.
Term: Two years. The House elects a chairperson called the ***Speaker of the House***.

How a Bill Becomes a Law

This chart shows a bill that starts in the House of Representatives, but it would follow the same steps if it were introduced in the Senate. A bill may start in the House or the Senate, or it may be introduced in both houses at the same time. Only bills that require spending money must begin in the House of Representatives.

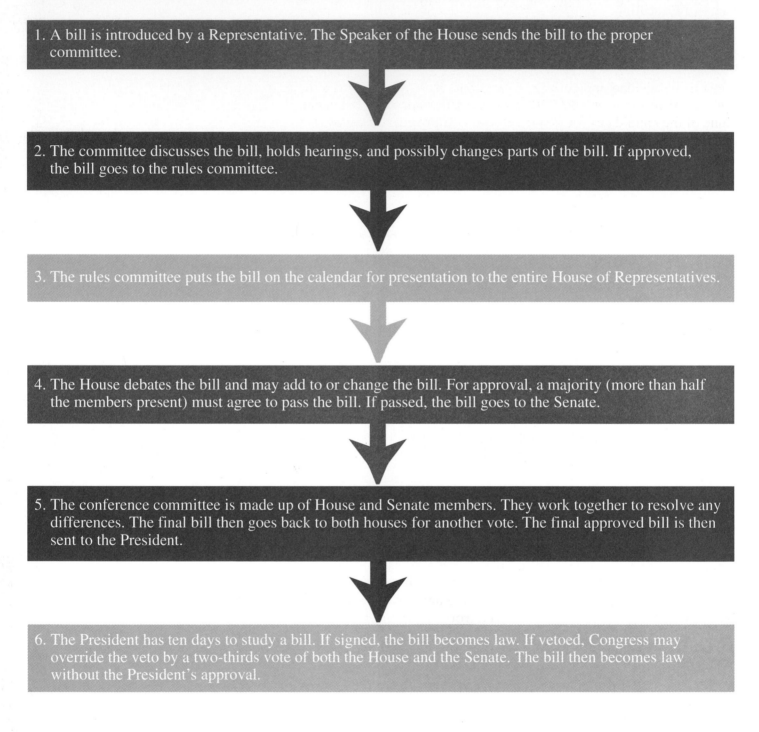

1. A bill is introduced by a Representative. The Speaker of the House sends the bill to the proper committee.

2. The committee discusses the bill, holds hearings, and possibly changes parts of the bill. If approved, the bill goes to the rules committee.

3. The rules committee puts the bill on the calendar for presentation to the entire House of Representatives.

4. The House debates the bill and may add to or change the bill. For approval, a majority (more than half the members present) must agree to pass the bill. If passed, the bill goes to the Senate.

5. The conference committee is made up of House and Senate members. They work together to resolve any differences. The final bill then goes back to both houses for another vote. The final approved bill is then sent to the President.

6. The President has ten days to study a bill. If signed, the bill becomes law. If vetoed, Congress may override the veto by a two-thirds vote of both the House and the Senate. The bill then becomes law without the President's approval.

The Electoral College System

The President and Vice President are chosen by the *electoral college*. The electoral college is not a school but a collection of electors (people) chosen by voters in each state. Each state has as many electors as the total number of its Representatives and Senators in Congress. For example, the state of New Jersey has thirteen Representatives and two Senators, making a total of fifteen. Therefore, New Jersey has fifteen electors, or electoral votes. A Presidential candidate must win a majority (more than half the votes) in the state. The majority winner then gets all of the electoral votes for that state. There are 538 total electors in the electoral college. A candidate must also receive a majority of the electoral votes, or at least 270 votes, in order to become President.

If none of the candidates for President and Vice President receives a majority of electoral votes, the choice goes to the House of Representatives. The House votes, with each state having one vote. To be elected President, a majority vote is needed.

 Only twice have the Presidential elections been sent to the House— the first in 1800 when Thomas Jefferson defeated Aaron Burr and the second in 1824 when John Quincy Adams won over Andrew Jackson and William H. Crawford.

 Twice the President-elect won the electoral vote but did not get the most popular votes, the first in 1876 when Rutherford B. Hayes was elected and the second in 1888 when Benjamin Harrison was elected.

IMPEACHMENT

The Constitution gives Congress the power to try a President of the United States who is accused of treason, bribery, or other high crimes. The House of Representatives may accuse, or *impeach*, the President. The Vice President, judges of U.S. courts, and Cabinet officers may also be impeached if they are accused of crimes.

The trial is held in the Senate. The accused may be convicted or judged not guilty. Two-thirds of the Senate must vote against the accused in order to convict. The penalty is being removed from office and never being allowed to hold a federal office again.

Note: The only President to be impeached was *Andrew Johnson* (see p. 70), but the Senate did not convict him. Johnson remained in office until the end of his term.

3 Declaration of Independence

This is the full text of the document written by Thomas Jefferson and signed in Philadelphia in 1776 (see p. 23).

(see p. 23)

When, in the course of human events, it becomes necessary for one people to dissolve the political bands which have connected them with another, and to assume, among the powers of the earth, the separate and equal station to which the laws of nature and of nature's God entitle them, a decent respect to the opinions of mankind requires that they should declare the causes which impel them to the separation.

We hold these truths to be self-evident: that all men are created equal; that they are endowed by their Creator with certain unalienable rights; that among these are life, liberty, and the pursuit of happiness. That, to secure these rights, governments are instituted among men, deriving their just powers from the consent of the governed; that, whenever any form of government becomes destructive of these ends, it is the right of the people to alter or to abolish it, and to institute a new government, laying its foundation on such principles, and organizing its powers in such form as to them shall seem most likely to effect their safety and happiness. Prudence, indeed, will dictate that governments long established should not be changed for light and transient causes; and accordingly all experience hath shown that mankind are more disposed to suffer while evils are sufferable, than to right themselves by abolishing the forms to which they are accustomed. But when a long train of abuses and usurpations, pursuing invariably the same object, evinces a design to reduce them under absolute despotism, it is their right, it is their duty, to throw off such government, and to provide new guards for their future security. Such has been the patient sufferance of these colonies; and such is now the necessity which constrains them to alter their former systems of government. The history of the present King of Great Britain is a history of repeated injuries and usurpations, all having in direct object the establishment of an absolute tyranny over these states. To prove this, let facts be submitted to a candid world.

He has refused his assent to laws the most wholesome and necessary for the public good.

He has forbidden his governors to pass laws of immediate and pressing importance, unless suspended in their operation till his assent should be obtained; and when so suspended, he has utterly neglected to attend to them.

He has refused to pass other laws for the accommodation of large districts of people, unless those people would relinquish the right of representation in the legislature, a right inestimable to them, and formidable to tyrants only.

He has called together legislative bodies at places unusual, uncomfortable, and distant from the depository of their public records, for the sole purpose of fatiguing them into compliance with his measures.

He has dissolved representative houses repeatedly for opposing, with manly firmness, his invasions on the rights of the people.

He has refused, for a long time after such dissolutions, to cause others to be elected, whereby the legislative powers, incapable of annihilation, have returned to the people at large for their exercise; the state remaining, in the mean time, exposed to all the dangers of invasions from without and convulsions within.

He has endeavored to prevent the population of these states; for that purpose obstructing the laws for the naturalization of foreigners, refusing to pass others to encourage their migration hither, and raising the conditions of new appropriations of lands.

He has obstructed the administration of justice, by refusing his assent to laws for establishing judiciary powers.

He has made judges dependent on his will alone for the tenure of their offices, and the amount and payment of their salaries.

He has erected a multitude of new offices, and sent hither swarms of officers to harass our people and eat out their substance.

He has kept among us, in times of peace, standing armies, without the consent of our legislatures.

He has affected to render the military independent of, and superior to, the civil power.

He has combined with others to subject us to a jurisdiction foreign to our constitutions and unacknowledged by our laws, giving his assent to their acts of pretended legislation:

For quartering large bodies of armed troops among us;

For protecting them, by a mock trial, from punishment for any murders which they should commit on the inhabitants of these states;

For cutting off our trade with all parts of the world;

For imposing taxes on us without our consent;

For depriving us, in many cases, of the benefits of trial by jury;

For transporting us beyond seas, to be tried for pretended offenses;

For abolishing the free system of English laws in a neighboring province, establishing therein an arbitrary government, and enlarging its boundaries, so as to render it at once an example and fit instrument for introducing the same absolute rule into these colonies;

For taking away our charters, abolishing our most valuable laws, and altering, fundamentally, the forms of our governments;

For suspending our own legislatures, and declaring themselves invested with power to legislate for us in all cases whatsoever.

He has abdicated government here, by declaring us out of his protection and waging war against us.

He has plundered our seas, ravaged our coasts, burned our towns, and destroyed the lives of our people.

He is at this time transporting large armies of foreign mercenaries to complete the works of death, desolation, and tyranny already begun with circumstances of cruelty and perfidy scarcely paralleled in the most barbarous ages, and totally unworthy the head of a civilized nation.

He has constrained our fellow-citizens, taken captive on the high seas, to bear arms against their country, to become the executioners of their friends and brethren, or to fall themselves by their hands.

He has excited domestic insurrection among us, and has endeavored to bring on the inhabitants of our frontiers the merciless Indian savages, whose known rule of warfare is an undistinguished destruction of all ages, sexes, and conditions.

In every stage of these oppressions we have petitioned for redress in the most humble terms; our repeated petitions have been answered only by repeated injury. A prince whose character is thus marked by every act which may define a tyrant is unfit to be the ruler of a free people.

Nor have we been wanting in our attentions to our British brethren. We have warned them, from time to time, of attempts by their legislature to extend an unwarrantable jurisdiction over us. We have reminded them of the circumstances of our emigration and settlement here. We have appealed to their native justice and magnanimity; and we have conjured them, by the ties of our common kindred, to disavow these usurpations, which would inevitably interrupt our connections and correspondence. They, too, have been deaf to the voice of justice and consanguinity. We must, therefore, acquiesce in the necessity which denounces our separation, and hold them as we hold the rest of mankind, enemies in war, in peace friends.

We, therefore, the representatives of the United States of America, in General Congress assembled, appealing to the Supreme Judge of the world for the rectitude of our intentions, do, in the name and by the authority of the good people of these colonies, solemnly publish and declare, That these united colonies are, and of right ought to be, free and independent states; that they are absolved from all allegiance to the British crown, and that all political connection between them and the state of Great Britain is, and ought to be, totally dissolved; and that, as free and independent states, they have full power to levy war, conclude peace, contract alliances, establish commerce, and do all other acts and things which independent states may of right do. And, for the support of this declaration, with a firm reliance on the protection of Divine Providence, we mutually pledge to each other our lives, our fortunes, and our sacred honor.

4 American Presidents

	PRESIDENT	VICE PRESIDENT	TERM	FIRST LADY
1.	George Washington	John Adams	1789-1797	Martha Washington
2.	John Adams	Thomas Jefferson	1797-1801	Abigail Smith Adams
3.	Thomas Jefferson	Aaron Burr George Clinton	1801-1805 1805-1809	Martha Skelton Jefferson
4.	James Madison	George Clinton Elbridge Gerry	1809-1813 1813-1817	Dorothea (Dolley) Madison
5.	James Monroe	Daniel D. Tompkins	1817-1825	Elizabeth Kortright Monroe
6.	John Quincy Adams	John C. Calhoun	1825-1829	Louisa Johnson Adams
7.	Andrew Jackson	John C. Calhoun Martin Van Buren	1829-1833 1833-1837	Rachel Donelson Jackson
8.	Martin Van Buren	Richard M. Johnson	1837-1841	Hannah Hoes Van Buren
9.	William Henry Harrison	John Tyler	3/1841-4/1841	Anna Symmes Harrison
10.	John Tyler		1841-1845	Julia Gardiner Tyler
11.	James K. Polk	George M. Dallas	1845-1849	Sarah Childress Polk
12.	Zachary Taylor	Millard Fillmore	3/1849-7/1850	Margaret Smith Taylor
13.	Millard Fillmore		1850-1853	Abigail Powers Fillmore
14.	Franklin Pierce	William R. King	1853-1857	Jane Appleton Pierce
15.	James Buchanan	John C. Breckinridge	1857-1861	None
16.	Abraham Lincoln	Hannibal Hamlin Andrew Johnson	1861-1865 3/1865-4/1865	Mary Todd Lincoln
17.	Andrew Johnson		1865-1869	Eliza McCardle Johnson
18.	Ulysses S. Grant	Schuyler Colfax Henry Wilson	1869-1873 1873-1877	Julia Dent Grant
19.	Rutherford B. Hayes	William A. Wheeler	1877-1881	Lucy Webb Hayes
20.	James Garfield	Chester A. Arthur	3/1881-9/1881	Lucretia Rudolph Garfield
21.	Chester A. Arthur		1881-1885	Ellen Herndon Arthur

PRESIDENT	VICE PRESIDENT	TERM	FIRST LADY
22. Grover Cleveland	Thomas A. Hendricks	1885-1889	Frances Folsom Cleveland
23. Benjamin Harrison	Levi P. Morton	1889-1893	Caroline Scott Harrison
24. Grover Cleveland	Adlai E. Stevenson	1893-1897	Frances Folsom Cleveland
25. William McKinley	Garret A. Hobart Theodore Roosevelt	1897-1901 3/1901-9/1901	Ida Saxton McKinley
26. Theodore Roosevelt	Charles W. Fairbanks	1901-1905 1905-1909	Edith Carow Roosevelt
27. William H. Taft	James S. Sherman	1909-1913	Helen Herron Taft
28. Woodrow Wilson	Thomas R. Marshall	1913-1917 1917-1921	Ellen Louise Axson Wilson (d.1914) Edith Bolling Galt Wilson
29. Warren G. Harding	Calvin Coolidge	3/1921-8/1923	Florence DeWolfe Harding
30. Calvin Coolidge	 Charles G. Dawes	1923-1925 1925-1929	Grace Goodhue Coolidge
31. Herbert C. Hoover	Charles Curtis	1929-1933	Lou Henry Hoover
32. Franklin D. Roosevelt	John N. Garner Henry A. Wallace Harry S Truman	1933-1941 1941-1945 1/1945-4/1945	Eleanor Roosevelt
33. Harry S Truman	 Albert W. Barkley	1945-1949 1949-1953	Elizabeth (Bess) Wallace Truman
34. Dwight D. Eisenhower	Richard M. Nixon	1953-1961	Marie (Mamie) Eisenhower
35. John F. Kennedy	Lyndon B. Johnson	1/1961-11/1963	Jacqueline Bouvier Kennedy
36. Lyndon B. Johnson Hubert H. Humphrey	1965-1969	1963-1965 Johnson	Claudia (Lady Bird) Taylor
37. Richard M. Nixon	Spiro T. Agnew Gerald R. Ford	1969-1973 1/1973-8/1974	Thelma (Pat) Ryan Nixon
38. Gerald R. Ford	Nelson A. Rockefeller	1974-1977	Elizabeth (Betty) Warren Ford
39. James (Jimmy) Carter	Walter F. Mondale	1977-1981	Rosalynn Smith Carter
40. Ronald Reagan	George Bush George Bush	1981-1985 1985-1989	Nancy Davis Reagan
41. George Bush	J. Danforth Quayle	1989-1993	Barbara Pierce Bush
42. William (Bill) Clinton	Albert Gore	1993-	Hillary Rodham Clinton

INDEX